Mastering Vulkan: From Fundamentals to Expert Techniques

Kameron Hussain and Frahaan Hussain

Published by Sonar Publishing, 2024.

MASTERING VULKAN: FROM FUNDAMENTALS TO EXPERT TECHNIQUES

First edition. December 9, 2024.

ISBN: 979-8230939351

Written by Kameron Hussain and Frahaan Hussain.

Mastering Vulkan

FROM FUNDAMENTALS TO EXPERT TECHNIQUES

FIRST EDITION

Preface

Graphics programming has undergone significant transformations in recent years, and Vulkan stands at the forefront of this evolution. As the demands for performance, efficiency, and control have increased, traditional graphics APIs have struggled to keep up. Vulkan, with its low-level access and explicit control over the GPU, has emerged as a powerful solution for developers who need to push the limits of modern hardware.

This book serves as a comprehensive guide to mastering Vulkan. Whether you're a game developer, a graphics engineer, or a researcher, the chapters ahead will help you understand and harness the power of this advanced API. We begin with an introduction to Vulkan, its history, and its core advantages over previous graphics APIs. From there, we explore setting up a development environment and dive deep into Vulkan's architecture, rendering techniques, and resource management.

Later chapters focus on advanced topics such as compute operations, debugging, and optimization. You'll also find insights on multi-platform development, real-world case studies, and future trends in graphics programming. Each chapter is structured to build upon the previous one, ensuring a smooth learning curve and a solid understanding of Vulkan's intricacies.

By the end of this book, you will have a robust knowledge of Vulkan and be equipped to build high-performance graphics applications. Whether you're rendering complex 3D scenes, creating compute-intensive applications, or optimizing performance for multiple platforms, this book will serve as your companion in mastering Vulkan.

We hope you find this book both informative and inspiring as you embark on your journey into the world of Vulkan.

Table of Contents

Chapter 1: Introduction to Vulkan

The Evolution of Graphics APIs

GRAPHICS PROGRAMMING has evolved significantly over the last few decades. As hardware has advanced and application complexity has increased, the demands on graphics APIs have grown substantially. To understand the context of Vulkan, it's essential to explore the evolution of graphics APIs, the limitations they encountered, and how Vulkan addresses these challenges.

Early Graphics APIs

IN THE EARLY DAYS OF computer graphics, APIs were relatively simple because hardware was less capable and applications had simpler rendering needs. Early APIs such as the *Graphics Language (GL)* and *DirectDraw* provided basic tools to draw shapes and images on the screen. These APIs abstracted the complexities of interacting with the GPU, providing straightforward, high-level functions to developers.

OpenGL

OPENGL, INTRODUCED in 1992, quickly became one of the most widely adopted graphics APIs. Developed by Silicon Graphics Inc., OpenGL provided a platform-independent interface to leverage 3D hardware acceleration. It featured a state-machine model that simplified many rendering tasks, making it popular among developers of games, simulations, and scientific visualizations.

However, as 3D graphics became more advanced, OpenGL began to show its age. The API's abstraction, while convenient, often led to performance bottlenecks. The driver model in OpenGL hid many details from the developer, resulting in unpredictable performance and limited control over GPU resources. This abstraction also introduced difficulties in multi-threading, as OpenGL was primarily designed to run on a single thread.

DirectX and Direct3D

MICROSOFT'S DIRECTX, which includes Direct3D, was another significant milestone in graphics programming. Launched in the mid-1990s, Direct3D provided developers with a powerful interface to take advantage of the Windows operating system's hardware capabilities. Unlike OpenGL, Direct3D evolved with tighter integration with Windows, offering developers features that leveraged the latest advancements in GPU hardware.

Direct3D improved upon some of OpenGL's limitations by offering a more predictable and streamlined interface. However, it too faced challenges with increasing complexity and the need for lower-level control over hardware. As graphics workloads became more demanding, developers needed more explicit control over memory management, synchronization, and parallel execution.

The Need for a New Approach

BY THE 2010S, GRAPHICS applications were pushing hardware to its limits. High-performance applications, such as AAA games, VR experiences, and scientific simulations, required more control over GPU resources and better performance predictability. The traditional graphics APIs like OpenGL and Direct3D 11 were struggling to keep up with these demands for several reasons:

1. **Driver Overhead**: The abstraction layers in traditional

APIs introduced significant overhead. Drivers had to make assumptions about how developers intended to use resources, which often led to inefficient execution paths.

2. **Single-Threaded Bottlenecks**: The reliance on a single-threaded command submission model limited the ability to exploit modern multi-core CPUs effectively. As CPUs gained more cores, developers needed ways to distribute graphics work across multiple threads.
3. **Lack of Explicit Control**: Traditional APIs hid much of the hardware's behavior from developers, making it difficult to optimize performance. Developers had limited visibility and control over how GPU memory and command execution were managed.
4. **Complexity in Resource Management**: Automatic resource management by drivers often led to unpredictable performance and inefficient memory usage.

Enter Vulkan

VULKAN, RELEASED BY the Khronos Group in 2016, was designed to address these challenges by providing a modern, low-level graphics API. Vulkan's design focuses on giving developers explicit control over GPU operations, memory management, and synchronization. This approach reduces driver overhead and allows developers to fully exploit the capabilities of modern hardware.

Key innovations in Vulkan include:

- **Low-Level Control**: Vulkan exposes the underlying hardware to developers, allowing for fine-grained control over resources and execution.

- **Multi-Threading Support**: Vulkan's design supports multi-threaded command submission, enabling developers to distribute work across multiple CPU cores effectively.

- **Explicit Synchronization**: Developers are responsible for managing synchronization, reducing the need for the driver to guess how resources are used.

- **Predictable Performance**: Because developers manage resources explicitly, Vulkan offers more predictable performance and eliminates much of the guesswork involved in driver optimization.

Comparing Vulkan to OpenGL and Direct3D

TO FULLY APPRECIATE Vulkan's advantages, it's helpful to compare it to OpenGL and Direct3D 11.

Feature	OpenGL	Direct3D 11	Vulkan
Abstraction Level	High	High	Low
Threading Model	Single-threaded	Single-threaded	Multi-threaded
Resource Management	Driver-managed	Driver-managed	Developer-managed
Performance Predictability	Low	Medium	High
Hardware Control	Limited	Moderate	Full
API Complexity	Low to Moderate	Moderate	High

The Role of Vulkan in Modern Graphics

VULKAN REPRESENTS A shift in how developers interact with GPU hardware. While the API is more complex and requires more effort to master, it offers unparalleled performance and control. This makes Vulkan especially valuable for:

- **Game Development**: Modern games demand high frame rates, low latency, and advanced rendering techniques. Vulkan's low-level access helps developers achieve these goals.

- **Virtual Reality (VR)**: VR applications require extremely low latency and consistent frame rates to provide a smooth experience. Vulkan's predictable performance is ideal for VR.

- **Scientific Visualization**: Large-scale visualizations benefit from Vulkan's ability to manage complex resources efficiently.

- **Compute-Intensive Applications**: Beyond graphics, Vulkan's compute capabilities enable developers to offload workloads to the GPU, such as AI processing and simulations.

As developers continue to push the boundaries of what's possible with graphics hardware, Vulkan will play a crucial role in enabling the next generation of applications.

Why Vulkan? Key Features and Advantages

VULKAN IS A MODERN, low-level graphics API that offers a range of features designed to address the performance and control limitations of its predecessors like OpenGL and Direct3D 11. By giving developers more explicit control over the GPU and associated resources, Vulkan provides a powerful platform for creating high-performance graphics applications. This section explores the core features and advantages of Vulkan, illustrating why it has become a preferred choice for modern graphics programming.

1. Explicit Control Over GPU Resources

ONE OF VULKAN'S STANDOUT features is the level of explicit control it gives developers over GPU resources. Unlike traditional APIs where drivers automatically manage resources, Vulkan requires developers to handle tasks like memory allocation, synchronization, and command submission.

This explicit control offers several advantages:

- **Predictable Performance**: Since developers manage resources directly, there are fewer surprises caused by the driver making assumptions. This leads to more consistent and predictable performance.
- **Efficient Resource Usage**: Developers can fine-tune memory allocations and buffer usage, minimizing wastage and optimizing performance for specific workloads.
- **Custom Resource Management**: Vulkan allows custom allocation strategies, which can be tailored for different types of applications, whether they are games, simulations, or compute workloads.

For example, in Vulkan, you allocate GPU memory explicitly using vkAllocateMemory:

```
VkMemoryAllocateInfo allocInfo = {};

allocInfo.sType = VK_STRUCTURE_TYPE_MEMORY_ALLOCATE_INFO;
```

```
allocInfo.allocationSize = 1024 * 1024; // Allocate 1 MB

allocInfo.memoryTypeIndex = FindMemoryType(physicalDevice, VK_MEMORY_PROPERTY_DEVICE_LOCAL_BIT);

VkDeviceMemory memory;

if (vkAllocateMemory(device, &allocInfo, nullptr, &memory) != VK_SUCCESS) {

throw std::runtime_error("Failed to allocate memory!");

}
```

This code snippet demonstrates how developers take direct control of memory allocation, specifying both the size and the type of memory.

2. Multi-Threading Support

TRADITIONAL APIS LIKE OpenGL have a single-threaded model for command submission, which often becomes a bottleneck in modern applications. Vulkan addresses this limitation by supporting multi-threaded command generation and submission.

In Vulkan, multiple threads can record command buffers concurrently, which can then be submitted to the GPU. This design allows applications to utilize multi-core CPUs more effectively.

Key components of Vulkan's multi-threading support include:

- **Command Buffers**: Command buffers are recorded independently and can be submitted from different threads.

- **Command Pools**: Each thread can manage its own command pool, allowing efficient allocation and recycling of command buffers.

- **Synchronization Primitives**: Vulkan provides fine-grained synchronization mechanisms like semaphores and fences to coordinate between threads and the GPU.

For example, you can create command pools for different threads:

```
VkCommandPoolCreateInfo poolInfo = {};

poolInfo.sType = VK_STRUCTURE_TYPE_COMMAND_POOL_CREATE_INFO;

poolInfo.queueFamilyIndex = graphicsQueueFamilyIndex;

poolInfo.flags = VK_COMMAND_POOL_CREATE_RESET_COMMAND_BUFFE

VkCommandPool commandPool;

if (vkCreateCommandPool(device, &poolInfo, nullptr, &commandPool) != VK_SUCCESS) {

throw std::runtime_error("Failed to create command pool!");

}
```

This enables each thread to record command buffers independently, significantly improving performance for multi-threaded applications.

3. Lower CPU Overhead

IN VULKAN, THE EXPLICIT nature of the API reduces the amount of work the CPU has to perform during draw calls and resource management. Unlike OpenGL, where the driver performs hidden state validation and optimizations, Vulkan minimizes driver intervention, allowing applications to achieve lower CPU overhead.

This reduction in CPU overhead results in:

- **Higher Performance for Draw-Call-Heavy Applications**: Applications that need to issue thousands of draw calls per frame benefit significantly from Vulkan's efficiency.

- **Improved Frame Rates**: By reducing CPU bottlenecks, Vulkan enables higher and more stable frame rates, especially in CPU-bound scenarios.

For example, Vulkan's command buffers allow multiple draw calls to be recorded and submitted in a single batch:

```
vkCmdBindPipeline(commandBuffer,
VK_PIPELINE_BIND_POINT_GRAPHICS, graphicsPipeline);

vkCmdDraw(commandBuffer, vertexCount, 1, 0, 0);
```

Since command buffers are pre-recorded and submitted in bulk, the CPU spends less time managing individual draw calls, leading to higher efficiency.

4. Advanced Synchronization Mechanisms

VULKAN REQUIRES DEVELOPERS to manage synchronization explicitly. While this adds complexity, it also offers greater control and efficiency. Vulkan provides synchronization primitives such as:

- **Semaphores**: Used to synchronize between GPU operations, such as ensuring a frame has finished rendering before presenting it to the screen.
- **Fences**: Used to synchronize between CPU and GPU operations, allowing the CPU to wait for the GPU to complete tasks.
- **Barriers**: Used to manage resource transitions, ensuring that memory is in the correct state before being accessed.

An example of using a fence to synchronize CPU-GPU operations:

```
VkFenceCreateInfo fenceInfo = {};

fenceInfo.sType = VK_STRUCTURE_TYPE_FENCE_CREATE_INFO;

VkFence fence;

if (vkCreateFence(device, &fenceInfo, nullptr, &fence) != VK_SUCCESS) {

throw std::runtime_error("Failed to create fence!");

}

vkQueueSubmit(graphicsQueue, 1, &submitInfo, fence);

vkWaitForFences(device, 1, &fence, VK_TRUE, UINT64_MAX);
```

This code ensures that the CPU waits until the GPU completes the submitted work, offering precise control over synchronization.

5. Cross-Platform Support

VULKAN IS A PLATFORM-agnostic API developed by the Khronos Group, making it a versatile choice for cross-platform development. Vulkan supports major operating systems, including:

- **Windows**: Full support for Windows applications.
- **Linux**: Native support for Linux-based systems.
- **Android**: Vulkan is the primary graphics API for Android, offering improved performance for mobile applications.
- **macOS and iOS**: Through the use of the *MoltenVK* library, Vulkan can run on Apple's platforms.

This cross-platform capability allows developers to write a single codebase that runs efficiently on multiple platforms, reducing development effort and maintenance costs.

6. Extensibility and Modern Features

VULKAN'S DESIGN ALLOWS for extensions that introduce new features without altering the core API. This extensibility ensures that Vulkan can adapt to new hardware capabilities and industry trends.

Some notable Vulkan features enabled through extensions include:

- **Ray Tracing**: Extensions like VK_KHR_ray_tracing_pipeline provide support for real-time ray tracing.
- **Mesh Shaders**: Support for advanced geometry processing through mesh and task shaders.

- **Variable Rate Shading (VRS)**: Allows developers to adjust the shading rate for different screen regions, improving performance without sacrificing visual quality.

For example, enabling a ray-tracing extension:

```
VkPhysicalDeviceRayTracingPipelineFeaturesKHR
rayTracingFeatures = {};

rayTracingFeatures.sType =
VK_STRUCTURE_TYPE_PHYSICAL_DEVICE_RAY_TRACING_

rayTracingFeatures.rayTracingPipeline = VK_TRUE;
```

7. Conclusion

VULKAN'S KEY FEATURES, such as explicit control, multi-threading, lower CPU overhead, advanced synchronization, and cross-platform support, make it a powerful choice for modern graphics programming. While Vulkan's complexity may seem daunting, the performance benefits and control it offers make it worth the investment for developers looking to push the boundaries of graphics applications.

By mastering Vulkan, developers gain the tools to create high-performance, efficient, and scalable graphics applications for a wide range of platforms and use cases.

Understanding Vulkan's Ecosystem

VULKAN'S ECOSYSTEM encompasses a wide range of tools, libraries, development kits, and community resources that support developers in creating high-performance graphics applications. This ecosystem provides the necessary infrastructure to streamline development, optimize performance, and debug applications efficiently. Understanding Vulkan's ecosystem is crucial to harnessing the full potential of this powerful graphics API.

1. Vulkan SDK

THE VULKAN SOFTWARE Development Kit (SDK) is the foundational toolset for Vulkan development. Maintained by LunarG, the Vulkan SDK includes everything a developer needs to get started with Vulkan, including libraries, headers, documentation, tools, and validation layers.

Components of the Vulkan SDK

1. **Vulkan Loader**: The loader handles the discovery and management of Vulkan drivers and layers. It abstracts away the specifics of loading different drivers on various platforms.

2. **Validation Layers**: These are essential tools for debugging and ensuring your Vulkan code follows best practices. Validation layers help catch errors during development by checking API calls, resource usage, and synchronization.

3. **Shader Tools**:

○ **GLSLang**: A compiler for GLSL (OpenGL Shading Language) shaders.

○ **SPIR-V Tools**: Tools for compiling, optimizing, and disassembling SPIR-V (Standard Portable Intermediate Representation) shaders.

4. **Debugging Tools**:

○ **Vulkan Configurator (vkconfig)**: A graphical tool for managing validation layers and debug configurations.

○ **RenderDoc**: An open-source graphics debugger that integrates with Vulkan for frame capture and analysis.

5. **Code Samples and Tutorials**: The SDK includes sample projects that demonstrate common Vulkan use cases, such as initializing a Vulkan instance, rendering a triangle, and managing resources.

Installing the Vulkan SDK

THE VULKAN SDK CAN be downloaded from the LunarG website for different platforms (Windows, Linux, and macOS). Once installed, you can set up the environment variables to use the Vulkan tools:

For Windows:

set VULKAN_SDK=C:\VulkanSDK\<version>\Bin

For Linux:

export VULKAN_SDK=/path/to/VulkanSDK/<version>/x86_64

2. Vulkan Layers

VULKAN LAYERS ARE OPTIONAL components that sit between the application and the Vulkan driver. They can intercept and modify Vulkan API calls for debugging, profiling, and validation purposes.

Types of Layers

1. **Validation Layers**: Provided by the Vulkan SDK, these layers check API usage and report errors or warnings. For example, they can detect invalid memory access, improper synchronization, and incorrect command buffer usage.
2. **Debug Layers**: These layers provide additional logging and debugging functionality, making it easier to track down issues in your Vulkan application.
3. **Profiling Layers**: Used to measure performance metrics and identify bottlenecks. Tools like NVIDIA Nsight and AMD Radeon GPU Profiler use custom layers to gather performance data.

Enabling Validation Layers

TO ENABLE VALIDATION layers in your application, you specify them during instance creation:

```
const char* validationLayers[] = {

"VK_LAYER_KHRONOS_validation"

};

VkInstanceCreateInfo createInfo = {};

createInfo.sType = VK_STRUCTURE_TYPE_INSTANCE_CREATE_INFO;

createInfo.enabledLayerCount = 1;

createInfo.ppEnabledLayerNames = validationLayers;
```

```
if (vkCreateInstance(&createInfo, nullptr, &instance) != VK_SUCCESS) {

throw std::runtime_error("Failed to create instance with validation layers!");

}
```

3. SPIR-V and Shading Languages

VULKAN USES SPIR-V as its intermediate shader representation. Unlike OpenGL, which compiles GLSL shaders at runtime, Vulkan requires shaders to be precompiled to SPIR-V before being used.

Writing Shaders in GLSL

YOU TYPICALLY WRITE shaders in GLSL and compile them to SPIR-V using glslangValidator:

Example vertex shader (shader.vert):

```
#version 450

layout(location = 0) in vec2 inPosition;

layout(location = 1) in vec3 inColor;

layout(location = 0) out vec3 fragColor;

void main() {

gl_Position = vec4(inPosition, 0.0, 1.0);

fragColor = inColor;

}
```

Compile to SPIR-V:

```
glslangValidator -V shader.vert -o shader.vert.spv
```

Using SPIR-V in Vulkan

IN YOUR VULKAN APPLICATION, load the SPIR-V binary and create a shader module:

```
std::vector<char> code = readFile("shader.vert.spv");

VkShaderModuleCreateInfo createInfo = {};

createInfo.sType = VK_STRUCTURE_TYPE_SHADER_MODULE_CREATE_INFO;

createInfo.codeSize = code.size();

createInfo.pCode = reinterpret_cast<const uint32_t*>(code.data());

VkShaderModule shaderModule;

if (vkCreateShaderModule(device, &createInfo, nullptr, &shaderModule) != VK_SUCCESS) {

throw std::runtime_error("Failed to create shader module!");

}
```

4. Graphics Debugging Tools

DEBUGGING AND OPTIMIZING Vulkan applications can be challenging due to the complexity of the API. Fortunately, several tools are available to help developers diagnose issues and optimize performance.

RenderDoc

RENDERDOC IS A POWERFUL open-source graphics debugger that supports Vulkan. It allows developers to capture frames, inspect draw calls, and analyze resource usage.

To capture a frame with RenderDoc:

1. Launch your Vulkan application through the RenderDoc interface.
2. Press F12 to capture the current frame.
3. Inspect the frame in the RenderDoc interface, examining draw calls, buffers, and textures.

NVIDIA Nsight Graphics

NVIDIA NSIGHT GRAPHICS is a comprehensive tool for debugging and profiling Vulkan applications on NVIDIA GPUs. It provides advanced features like:

- **Frame Capture and Replay**: Capture a frame and replay it to analyze individual draw calls.

- **Performance Analysis**: Identify GPU bottlenecks and optimize resource usage.

- **Shader Debugging**: Step through shader code to debug complex rendering issues.

AMD Radeon GPU Profiler (RGP)

AMD'S RADEON GPU PROFILER helps developers analyze Vulkan applications on AMD hardware. It offers detailed profiling of GPU workloads, helping identify performance bottlenecks.

5. Community and Resources

THE VULKAN COMMUNITY plays a crucial role in supporting developers, sharing knowledge, and advancing the API. There are numerous resources where developers can seek help, learn, and contribute.

Khronos Group Forums

THE **Khronos Group Forums** are the official discussion boards for Vulkan-related topics. Developers can ask questions, report issues, and share solutions.

Vulkan Subreddit

THE **r/vulkan** subreddit is an active community where developers share news, tutorials, and troubleshooting advice.

GitHub Repositories

SEVERAL OPEN-SOURCE projects on GitHub provide Vulkan samples, tools, and libraries. Notable repositories include:

- **Sascha Willems' Vulkan Samples**: A collection of comprehensive Vulkan examples demonstrating various techniques.

- **Vulkan-Hpp**: A C++ header for Vulkan, offering a more idiomatic interface for C++ developers.

YouTube Tutorials

NUMEROUS YOUTUBE CHANNELS provide Vulkan tutorials, covering topics from basic setup to advanced rendering techniques. These video resources can be invaluable for visual learners.

6. Conclusion

VULKAN'S ECOSYSTEM is a rich and evolving landscape of tools, libraries, and community resources designed to support developers in creating high-performance graphics applications. The Vulkan SDK, validation layers, debugging tools, and community resources provide everything you need to navigate Vulkan's complexities and build robust, efficient applications. By leveraging these tools, you can streamline development, catch errors early, and optimize your application for maximum performance.

Chapter 2: Setting Up Your Development Environment

System Requirements and Tools

BEFORE DIVING INTO Vulkan development, it's essential to ensure that your system meets the necessary requirements and that you have the right tools installed. Vulkan, being a low-level graphics API, has specific hardware and software dependencies that developers must address to create efficient, high-performance applications.

Hardware Requirements

TO WORK WITH VULKAN, your system must have a GPU that supports the Vulkan API. Vulkan compatibility is primarily determined by the GPU vendor and the specific model. Here's a summary of supported hardware by major GPU manufacturers:

- **NVIDIA**: Vulkan is supported on most modern NVIDIA GPUs starting from the GeForce 600 series (Kepler architecture) and newer.

- **AMD**: Radeon GPUs from the GCN 1.0 architecture (Radeon HD 7000 series) and newer support Vulkan.

- **Intel**: Integrated GPUs starting from Intel's HD Graphics 500 series (Skylake architecture) support Vulkan.

- **Mobile GPUs**: Many modern mobile GPUs from vendors like ARM (Mali), Qualcomm (Adreno), and Imagination Technologies (PowerVR) support Vulkan.

You can check the compatibility of your GPU by visiting the official website of your GPU vendor or using tools like **GPU-Z** (for Windows) and **glxinfo** (for Linux).

Operating System Requirements

VULKAN IS A CROSS-PLATFORM API, and you can develop applications on multiple operating systems, including:

- **Windows** (Windows 7, 8, 10, 11)
- **Linux** (most distributions like Ubuntu, Fedora, and Arch)
- **macOS** (through the MoltenVK library)
- **Android** (version 6.0 Marshmallow and newer)

Ensure that your operating system is updated to the latest version to avoid compatibility issues with Vulkan drivers and tools.

Vulkan Drivers

INSTALLING THE APPROPRIATE Vulkan drivers is crucial for development. GPU vendors provide drivers that enable Vulkan support. You can download the latest Vulkan-compatible drivers from the following sources:

- **NVIDIA**:NVIDIA Driver Download[1]
- **AMD**: AMD Driver Download
- **Intel**: Intel Graphics Drivers

1. https://www.nvidia.com/Download/index.aspx

After installing the drivers, verify that Vulkan is correctly installed by running the following command:

On Windows (using vulkaninfo):

vulkaninfo

On Linux:

vulkaninfo | less

This will provide detailed information about your Vulkan installation, including supported devices, extensions, and layers.

Essential Development Tools

TO SET UP A VULKAN development environment, you need several tools. Here's a list of essential tools and libraries you'll need:

1. **Vulkan SDK**: The Vulkan Software Development Kit (SDK) provides headers, libraries, and tools necessary for Vulkan development.

2. **C++ Compiler**: Most Vulkan projects are developed in C++. Popular compilers include:

   ○ **Windows**: Microsoft Visual C++ (MSVC), MinGW

   ○ **Linux**: GCC, Clang

3. **Build System**: Tools like CMake, Make, or Visual Studio project files help manage and build your project.

4. **IDE/Code Editor**: Popular IDEs for Vulkan development include Visual Studio, CLion, and Visual Studio Code.

5. **Debugger**: Tools like gdb (GNU Debugger) and Visual Studio's built-in debugger help debug your application.

6. **Graphics Debugging Tools**:

○ **RenderDoc**: A powerful graphics debugger for Vulkan.

○ **NVIDIA Nsight**: Graphics debugging and profiling tool for NVIDIA GPUs.

○ **AMD Radeon GPU Profiler**: Profiling tool for AMD GPUs.

Installing Vulkan SDK

THE VULKAN SDK IS PROVIDED by **LunarG** and includes everything you need to develop and debug Vulkan applications. Follow these steps to install the Vulkan SDK on different platforms.

Installing Vulkan SDK on Windows

1. **Download the SDK**: Visit the official Vulkan SDK website: LunarG Vulkan SDK and download the latest version for Windows.

INSTALL THE SDK: Run the installer and follow the on-screen instructions. The default installation path is typically:

makefile

C:\VulkanSDK\<version>\

1.

Set Environment Variables: The installer typically sets environment variables automatically. To verify, open a Command Prompt and run:

bash

```
echo %VULKAN_SDK%
```

1. This should display the path to your Vulkan SDK installation.

Verify Installation: Open a Command Prompt and run:

bash

```
vulkaninfo
```

1. If vulkaninfo executes successfully and displays detailed information about your GPU, the installation is complete.

Installing Vulkan SDK on Linux

1. **Download the SDK**: Visit the Vulkan SDK website and download the latest SDK for Linux.

EXTRACT AND INSTALL: After downloading, extract the archive:

bash

```
tar -xzf vulkansdk-linux-x.x.x.x.tar.gz
```

1. Follow the installation instructions provided in the archive.

Set Environment Variables: Add the following lines to your ~/.bashrc or ~/.profile:

bash

export VULKAN_SDK=/path/to/vulkan-sdk/x.x.x.x/x86_64

export PATH=$VULKAN_SDK/bin:$PATH

export LD_LIBRARY_PATH=$VULKAN_SDK/lib:$LD_LIBRARY_PATH

export VK_ICD_FILENAMES=$VULKAN_SDK/etc/vulkan/icd.d

export VK_LAYER_PATH=$VULKAN_SDK/etc/vulkan/explicit_layer.d

Source the file:

bash

source ~/.bashrc

1.

Verify Installation: Run vulkaninfo:

bash

vulkaninfo | less

1.

Installing Vulkan SDK on macOS

VULKAN ISN'T NATIVELY supported on macOS, but you can use **MoltenVK**, a Vulkan-to-Metal translation layer.

Install via Homebrew:

bash

brew install molten-vk

1.

Set Environment Variables:

bash

export VULKAN_SDK=/usr/local

1.

Verify Installation:

bash

vulkaninfo

1.

Configuring Your Development Environment

AFTER INSTALLING THE Vulkan SDK, you need to configure your development environment to compile and run Vulkan projects.

Creating a Basic CMake Project

HERE'S A SAMPLE CMAKELISTS.txt for a basic Vulkan project:

cmake_minimum_required(VERSION 3.10)

project(BasicVulkanApp)

set(CMAKE_CXX_STANDARD 17)

find_package(Vulkan REQUIRED)

```
add_executable(basic_vulkan_app main.cpp)

target_include_directories(basic_vulkan_app PRIVATE ${Vulkan_INCLUDE_DIRS})

target_link_libraries(basic_vulkan_app PRIVATE ${Vulkan_LIBRARIES})
```

Sample main.cpp File

HERE'S A MINIMAL MAIN.cpp file to ensure your Vulkan setup works:

```
#include <vulkan/vulkan.h>

#include <iostream>

int main() {

uint32_t instanceExtensionCount = 0;

vkEnumerateInstanceExtensionProperties(nullptr, &instanceExtensionCount, nullptr);

std::cout << "Vulkan Instance Extension Count: " << instanceExtensionCount << std::endl;

return 0;

}
```

Building the Project

CREATE A BUILD DIRECTORY:

bash

mkdir build && cd build

1.

Run CMake:

bash

cmake ..

1.

Build the project:

bash

make

1.

Run the executable:

bash

./basic_vulkan_app

1.

If everything is set up correctly, the program should display the number of Vulkan instance extensions available.

This completes the setup of your Vulkan development environment. You are now ready to begin writing and experimenting with Vulkan code!

Installing Vulkan SDK

INSTALLING THE VULKAN Software Development Kit (SDK) is a crucial step for developing Vulkan applications. The SDK provides essential tools, libraries, headers, and documentation to help you create efficient Vulkan programs. This section will guide you through the installation process for Windows, Linux, and macOS, ensuring you have a fully functional Vulkan development environment.

What's Included in the Vulkan SDK?

THE VULKAN SDK, MAINTAINED by **LunarG**, is a comprehensive toolkit that includes:

1. **Vulkan Headers**: Header files (.h) necessary for including Vulkan functions in your code.

2. **Vulkan Libraries**: Static and dynamic libraries to link against your application.

3. **Tools**:

○ **vulkaninfo**: Displays detailed information about your Vulkan installation and system capabilities.

○ **Validation Layers**: Debugging tools to catch common mistakes and enforce best practices.

○ **glslangValidator**: A compiler for GLSL (OpenGL Shading Language) into SPIR-V, the binary format used by Vulkan shaders.

4. **Sample Code**: Reference implementations and example projects to get you started.

5. **Documentation**: Guides and API references to help you understand Vulkan's architecture and functions.

Now, let's go through the installation process for each platform.

Installing Vulkan SDK on Windows

Step 1: Download the Vulkan SDK

1. Visit the official Vulkan SDK website maintained by LunarG:
   LunarG Vulkan SDK Downloads
2. Select the **Windows** version of the SDK and download the installer. The latest versions are typically provided for both **64-bit** and **32-bit** systems. Ensure you download the correct version for your operating system.

Step 2: Run the Installer

1. Once the download is complete, run the installer executable (VulkanSDK-x.x.x.x-Installer.exe).
2. Follow the on-screen instructions, selecting the default options unless you have a specific installation path in mind.

THE INSTALLER WILL set up the SDK in a default directory, typically:

C:\VulkanSDK\<version>\

Step 3: Set Environment Variables

THE INSTALLER SHOULD automatically configure your system's environment variables. However, it's a good practice to verify that the environment variables are correctly set. The key variables include:

- **VULKAN_SDK**: Path to the installed Vulkan SDK.

- **PATH**: Includes the Vulkan SDK bin directory.
- **VK_ICD_FILENAMES**: Path to the Vulkan loader JSON files.
- **VK_LAYER_PATH**: Path to the validation layers.

To check these variables:

1. Open a **Command Prompt**.
2. Type the following commands:

```
echo %VULKAN_SDK%

echo %PATH%

echo %VK_ICD_FILENAMES%

echo %VK_LAYER_PATH%
```

Step 4: Verify the Installation

TO ENSURE THE VULKAN SDK is installed correctly, run vulkaninfo, a tool provided by the SDK:

```
vulkaninfo
```

If the tool executes successfully and displays detailed information about your Vulkan drivers, instance, and physical devices, your installation is complete.

Step 5: Install Visual Studio (Optional)

IF YOU PREFER USING **Microsoft Visual Studio** for Vulkan development:

1. Download and install **Visual Studio Community Edition** from theofficial website[2].
2. During installation, ensure you select the **Desktop development with C++** workload.
3. Open Visual Studio, create a new project, and ensure the Vulkan headers and libraries are included in your project settings.

Installing Vulkan SDK on Linux

Step 1: Download the Vulkan SDK

1. Visit the official LunarG website:
   LunarG Vulkan SDK Downloads
2. Download the **Linux** version of the SDK. The file will be a .tar.gz archive (e.g., vulkan-sdk-linux-x.x.x.x.tar.gz).

Step 2: Extract the SDK

EXTRACT THE DOWNLOADED archive to your desired installation directory:

```
tar -xzf vulkansdk-linux-x.x.x.x.tar.gz
```

Step 3: Set Environment Variables

TO MAKE THE VULKAN tools accessible, add the following environment variables to your shell configuration file (e.g., ~/.bashrc or ~/.zshrc):

```
export VULKAN_SDK=/path/to/vulkan-sdk/x.x.x.x/x86_64
```

2. https://visualstudio.microsoft.com/

export PATH=$VULKAN_SDK/bin:$PATH

export LD_LIBRARY_PATH=$VULKAN_SDK/lib:$LD_LIBRARY_PATH

export VK_ICD_FILENAMES=$VULKAN_SDK/etc/vulkan/icd.d

export VK_LAYER_PATH=$VULKAN_SDK/etc/vulkan/explicit_layer.d

Source the configuration file to apply the changes:

source ~/.bashrc

Step 4: Install Dependencies

ENSURE YOU HAVE THE necessary dependencies installed. For **Ubuntu** or **Debian**-based systems:

sudo apt-get update

sudo apt-get install build-essential cmake libx11-dev libx11-xcb-dev libxcb1-dev libx11-xcb-dev libxcb-icccm4-dev libxcb-image0-dev libxcb-randr0-dev libxcb-shape0-dev libxcb-shm0-dev libxcb-util0-dev libxcb-xfixes0-dev libxcb-xinerama0-dev libxcb-xkb-dev libxkbcommon-dev libxkbcommon-x11-dev libwayland-dev libxrandr-dev

Step 5: Verify Installation

RUN THE VULKANINFO tool to confirm the installation:

vulkaninfo | less

If the tool outputs detailed Vulkan information, the installation is successful.

Installing Vulkan SDK on macOS

MACOS DOES NOT SUPPORT Vulkan natively. However, you can use **MoltenVK**, a Vulkan-to-Metal translation layer that allows Vulkan applications to run on macOS.

Step 1: Install MoltenVK via Homebrew

INSTALL **MoltenVK** using Homebrew:

```
brew install molten-vk
```

Step 2: Set Environment Variables

ADD THE FOLLOWING LINES to your shell configuration file (e.g., ~/.zshrc or ~/.bash_profile):

```
export VULKAN_SDK=/usr/local

export PATH=$VULKAN_SDK/bin:$PATH
```

Source the file to apply changes:

```
source ~/.zshrc
```

Step 3: Verify Installation

CHECK IF VULKANINFO runs successfully:

```
vulkaninfo
```

Troubleshooting Installation Issues

Common Errors and Solutions

1. **vulkaninfo Not Found**:

   ○ Ensure that the PATH variable includes the Vulkan SDK bin directory.

   ○ Verify that the SDK installation completed without errors.

2. **Driver Issues**:

   ○ Ensure you have the latest GPU drivers installed.

   ○ For Linux, verify that your system uses the correct GPU driver (e.g., NVIDIA, AMD, or Mesa).

3. **Missing Environment Variables**:

   ○ Check if VULKAN_SDK and related variables are set correctly.

   ○ Reinstall the SDK if necessary.

4. **Permission Issues**:

   ○ On Linux and macOS, ensure you have execute permissions for Vulkan tools:

BASH

```
chmod +x $VULKAN_SDK/bin/*
```

5.

By following these steps, you should have a fully functional Vulkan SDK installed and ready for development on your chosen platform. You are now prepared to configure and create your first Vulkan project.

Configuring Your First Vulkan Project

SETTING UP A VULKAN project from scratch requires careful configuration of your build environment, project files, and dependencies. This section provides a step-by-step guide to configuring your first Vulkan project. By the end of this section, you'll have a minimal Vulkan application that compiles and runs, displaying basic information about your GPU and Vulkan instance.

Prerequisites for Configuration

BEFORE STARTING, ENSURE the following are installed on your system:

1. **Vulkan SDK**: Installed and verified (vulkaninfo works).

2. **C++ Compiler**:

  ○ **Windows**: Microsoft Visual C++ (MSVC) or MinGW.

  ○ **Linux**: GCC or Clang.

  ○ **macOS**: Clang (with MoltenVK).

3. **Build System**:

◦ **CMake** (recommended for cross-platform projects).

4. **IDE or Text Editor**: Visual Studio, CLion, or Visual Studio Code.

Step 1: Creating the Project Directory Structure

START BY CREATING A clean project directory structure:

```
VulkanProject/
│—CMakeLists.txt
│—src/
│  └── main.cpp
└—include/
└── (Optional header files)
```

- **CMakeLists.txt**: The build configuration file for CMake.
- **src/main.cpp**: The main source file where your Vulkan code will reside.
- **include/**: Optional directory for header files.

Step 2: Writing the CMakeLists.txt File

CREATE A CMAKELISTS.txt file at the root of your project directory. This file configures how CMake will build your project and link the Vulkan libraries.

```
cmake_minimum_required(VERSION 3.10)
```

```
project(VulkanProject)

# Set the C++ standard

set(CMAKE_CXX_STANDARD 17)

# Find Vulkan package

find_package(Vulkan REQUIRED)

# Add executable target

add_executable(VulkanProject src/main.cpp)

# Include Vulkan directories

target_include_directories(VulkanProject PRIVATE ${Vulkan_INCLUDE_DIRS})

# Link Vulkan libraries

target_link_libraries(VulkanProject PRIVATE ${Vulkan_LIBRARIES})
```

Explanation of CMakeLists.txt:

- **project(VulkanProject)**: Defines the project name.
- **set(CMAKE_CXX_STANDARD 17)**: Sets the C++ standard to C++17.
- **find_package(Vulkan REQUIRED)**: Searches for the Vulkan SDK and makes it available to the project.
- **add_executable(VulkanProject src/main.cpp)**: Adds the executable target with main.cpp as the source file.

- **target_include_directories**: Adds the Vulkan include directories to the project.
- **target_link_libraries**: Links the Vulkan libraries to the executable.

Step 3: Writing a Minimal Vulkan Program in main.cpp

CREATE SRC/MAIN.CPP and add the following minimal Vulkan code. This code initializes a Vulkan instance and queries the available physical devices.

```
#include <vulkan/vulkan.h>

#include <iostream>

#include <vector>

int main() {

// Create a Vulkan instance

VkInstance instance;

VkApplicationInfo appInfo{};

appInfo.sType =
VK_STRUCTURE_TYPE_APPLICATION_INFO;

appInfo.pApplicationName = "Minimal Vulkan App";

appInfo.applicationVersion = VK_MAKE_VERSION(1, 0, 0);

appInfo.pEngineName = "No Engine";

appInfo.engineVersion = VK_MAKE_VERSION(1, 0, 0);
```

```
appInfo.apiVersion = VK_API_VERSION_1_0;

VkInstanceCreateInfo createInfo{};

createInfo.sType =
VK_STRUCTURE_TYPE_INSTANCE_CREATE_INFO;

createInfo.pApplicationInfo = &appInfo;

if (vkCreateInstance(&createInfo, nullptr, &instance) !=
VK_SUCCESS) {

std::cerr << "Failed to create Vulkan instance!" << std::endl;

return EXIT_FAILURE;

}

std::cout << "Vulkan instance created successfully!" << std::endl;

// Enumerate physical devices (GPUs)

uint32_t deviceCount = 0;

vkEnumeratePhysicalDevices(instance, &deviceCount, nullptr);

if (deviceCount == 0) {

std::cerr << "Failed to find GPUs with Vulkan support!" <<
std::endl;

return EXIT_FAILURE;

}

std::vector<VkPhysicalDevice> devices(deviceCount);

vkEnumeratePhysicalDevices(instance, &deviceCount,
devices.data());
```

```
std::cout << "Found " << deviceCount << " GPU(s) with Vulkan support:" << std::endl;

for (const auto& device : devices) {

VkPhysicalDeviceProperties deviceProperties;

vkGetPhysicalDeviceProperties(device, &deviceProperties);

std::cout << "\t" << deviceProperties.deviceName << std::endl;

}

// Clean up Vulkan instance

vkDestroyInstance(instance, nullptr);

return EXIT_SUCCESS;

}
```

Code Breakdown:

1. **Vulkan Instance Creation**:
   - **VkApplicationInfo** provides application details.
   - **VkInstanceCreateInfo** is used to create the Vulkan instance.
   - **vkCreateInstance** initializes the Vulkan instance.
2. **Physical Device Enumeration**:
   - **vkEnumeratePhysicalDevices** queries the available GPUs.

○ **vkGetPhysicalDeviceProperties** retrieves properties like the device name.

3. **Cleanup**:

○ **vkDestroyInstance** destroys the Vulkan instance before exiting.

Step 4: Building the Project

Using CMake to Generate Build Files

OPEN A TERMINAL IN the root project directory and run the following commands:

```
mkdir build

cd build

cmake ..
```

This generates the necessary build files (Makefiles on Linux/macOS or Visual Studio project files on Windows).

Compiling the Project

ON LINUX OR MACOS, use make:

```
make
```

On Windows, if using Visual Studio:

1. Open the generated .sln file in Visual Studio.
2. Select **Build** -> **Build Solution**.

Step 5: Running the Project

AFTER COMPILING, YOU'LL have an executable named VulkanProject. Run it:

On Linux/macOS:

./VulkanProject

On Windows (Command Prompt):

VulkanProject.exe

Expected Output

IF EVERYTHING IS SET up correctly, you should see output similar to:

Vulkan instance created successfully!

Found 1 GPU(s) with Vulkan support:

NVIDIA GeForce GTX 1050 Ti

Debugging Tips

1. **Validation Layers:**

   ○ Use Vulkan's **validation layers** to catch mistakes during development.

ENABLE VALIDATION LAYERS by modifying the VkInstanceCreateInfo:

cpp

const char* validationLayers[] = { "VK_LAYER_KHRONOS_validation" };

createInfo.enabledLayerCount = 1;

createInfo.ppEnabledLayerNames = validationLayers;

○

2. **Common Issues**:

○ **Missing Vulkan Drivers**: Ensure you have the latest GPU drivers.

○ **Environment Variables**: Verify VULKAN_SDK is set correctly.

○ **Permissions**: On Linux, ensure you have permission to access GPU devices.

Conclusion

YOU HAVE SUCCESSFULLY configured and built your first Vulkan project. This minimal example demonstrates the essential steps for setting up Vulkan, creating an instance, and enumerating GPUs. You are now ready to explore more advanced Vulkan features, such as creating swapchains, command buffers, and rendering pipelines.

Chapter 3: Vulkan Architecture and Workflow

Vulkan's Core Concepts

IN ORDER TO HARNESS the full potential of Vulkan, it is crucial to understand the fundamental concepts that form the backbone of this modern graphics API. Vulkan differs significantly from older APIs like OpenGL in terms of design philosophy, performance, and control. This section delves into these core concepts, highlighting the principles that guide Vulkan's operation and providing a detailed exploration of the key elements that developers need to grasp to create efficient, high-performance graphics applications.

Core Design Philosophy

VULKAN WAS DESIGNED with a set of core principles that address the limitations of older graphics APIs. These principles ensure that developers have maximum control over the hardware, which is essential for optimizing performance in modern applications.

1. **Explicit Control**: Unlike OpenGL, which abstracts many details away, Vulkan gives developers explicit control over the GPU and its operations. This means developers are responsible for managing resources, synchronization, and command execution.
2. **Low Overhead**: Vulkan minimizes CPU overhead by reducing the number of driver-related tasks. This allows for lower-level access to the GPU and improves performance, especially in applications that render complex scenes or

manage large datasets.

3. **Parallelism**: Vulkan is designed to take full advantage of multi-core CPUs. By providing mechanisms to issue commands in parallel, Vulkan allows developers to better utilize modern hardware architectures.
4. **Predictable Performance**: Vulkan aims to deliver consistent, predictable performance by reducing the chances of unexpected driver behavior. This helps developers avoid pitfalls like "driver magic" and hidden optimizations that can vary between implementations.
5. **Cross-Platform Compatibility**: Vulkan is a platform-agnostic API. Applications built with Vulkan can run on multiple operating systems and devices, including Windows, Linux, Android, and more.

Key Components of Vulkan

TO EFFECTIVELY USE Vulkan, developers need to understand its key components. These building blocks provide the structure through which Vulkan operates.

1. **Instance**: The instance represents the connection between the application and the Vulkan library. It encapsulates the state necessary to initialize and interact with the Vulkan API.
2. **Physical Device**: A physical device represents the GPU hardware. In Vulkan, you can enumerate multiple physical devices and choose the one that best suits your needs. Each physical device has specific properties, such as available memory, supported features, and queue families.
3. **Logical Device**: A logical device is an abstraction of a physical device that allows you to interact with the GPU.

The logical device provides access to the GPU's resources through interfaces known as **queues**.

4. **Queues**: Queues are used to submit commands to the GPU. Vulkan supports different types of queues, such as graphics, compute, and transfer queues. Developers must explicitly manage how commands are sent to these queues to optimize performance.
5. **Command Buffers**: Command buffers store the commands that will be sent to the GPU. This enables batch processing and reduces the CPU overhead associated with issuing individual commands.
6. **Pipeline**: The pipeline defines the sequence of operations that the GPU will execute. Vulkan uses **graphics pipelines** for rendering operations and **compute pipelines** for non-graphics tasks. The pipeline configuration must be specified in detail before execution.
7. **Swapchain**: The swapchain manages the presentation of images to the screen. It handles the buffers that are displayed and ensures that the rendering and presentation processes are synchronized.

Vulkan Initialization Workflow

VULKAN'S INITIALIZATION process consists of several steps that need to be carefully followed to set up a functional rendering context. The steps are as follows:

1. **Create a Vulkan Instance**: Initialize a VkInstance to establish a connection with the Vulkan API.
2. **Select a Physical Device**: Enumerate available physical devices and choose one based on desired capabilities and features.

3. **Create a Logical Device and Queues**: Create a VkDevice and specify the queue families to enable graphics, compute, or transfer operations.
4. **Set Up the Swapchain**: Create a swapchain to manage image presentation to the screen.
5. **Create Command Buffers and Command Pools**: Allocate command buffers to record drawing and resource management commands.
6. **Set Up the Graphics Pipeline**: Define the graphics pipeline stages, including shaders, vertex input, rasterization, and output stages.
7. **Allocate Buffers and Images**: Create buffers and images to store vertex data, textures, and other resources.
8. **Synchronization Objects**: Set up synchronization primitives like semaphores and fences to manage command execution flow.

Let's explore these steps in more detail with code snippets where applicable.

---

1. Creating a Vulkan Instance

THE FIRST STEP IN SETTING up Vulkan is creating a VkInstance. The instance initializes the connection between your application and the Vulkan library.

VkApplicationInfo appInfo = {};

appInfo.sType = VK_STRUCTURE_TYPE_APPLICATION_INFO;

appInfo.pApplicationName = "VulkanApp";

appInfo.applicationVersion = VK_MAKE_VERSION(1, 0, 0);

```
appInfo.pEngineName = "No Engine";

appInfo.engineVersion = VK_MAKE_VERSION(1, 0, 0);

appInfo.apiVersion = VK_API_VERSION_1_0;

VkInstanceCreateInfo createInfo = {};

createInfo.sType = VK_STRUCTURE_TYPE_INSTANCE_CREATE_INFO;

createInfo.pApplicationInfo = &appInfo;

if (vkCreateInstance(&createInfo, NULL, &instance) != VK_SUCCESS) {

printf("Failed to create Vulkan instance!\n");

}
```

In this snippet:

- VkApplicationInfo contains metadata about your application.
- VkInstanceCreateInfo specifies the parameters for creating the instance.
- vkCreateInstance initializes the instance.

---

2. Selecting a Physical Device

AFTER CREATING THE instance, the next step is selecting a physical device. Here's how you can enumerate the available GPUs:

```
uint32_t deviceCount = 0;
```

```
vkEnumeratePhysicalDevices(instance, &deviceCount, NULL);

VkPhysicalDevice devices[deviceCount];

vkEnumeratePhysicalDevices(instance, &deviceCount, devices);

for (uint32_t i = 0; i < deviceCount; i++) {

VkPhysicalDeviceProperties deviceProperties;

vkGetPhysicalDeviceProperties(devices[i], &deviceProperties);

printf("Device Name: %s\n", deviceProperties.deviceName);

}
```

This code retrieves a list of physical devices and prints their names.

3. Creating a Logical Device

ONCE A SUITABLE PHYSICAL device is selected, create a logical device and specify the queues you'll use:

```
VkDeviceQueueCreateInfo queueCreateInfo = {};

queueCreateInfo.sType = VK_STRUCTURE_TYPE_DEVICE_QUEUE_CREATE_INFO;

queueCreateInfo.queueFamilyIndex = 0;

queueCreateInfo.queueCount = 1;

float queuePriority = 1.0f;

queueCreateInfo.pQueuePriorities = &queuePriority;

VkDeviceCreateInfo deviceCreateInfo = {};
```

deviceCreateInfo.sType = VK_STRUCTURE_TYPE_DEVICE_CREATE_INFO;

deviceCreateInfo.queueCreateInfoCount = 1;

deviceCreateInfo.pQueueCreateInfos = &queueCreateInfo;

VkDevice device;

if (vkCreateDevice(physicalDevice, &deviceCreateInfo, NULL, &device) != VK_SUCCESS) {

printf("Failed to create logical device!\n");

}

This snippet:

- Creates a queue with a priority of 1.0.
- Initializes the logical device with the queue configuration.

---

4. Command Buffers and Pools

COMMAND BUFFERS ARE allocated from a command pool. Here's an example:

VkCommandPoolCreateInfo poolInfo = {};

poolInfo.sType = VK_STRUCTURE_TYPE_COMMAND_POOL_CREATE_INFO;

poolInfo.queueFamilyIndex = 0;

VkCommandPool commandPool;

```
vkCreateCommandPool(device, &poolInfo, NULL, &commandPool);

VkCommandBufferAllocateInfo allocInfo = {};

allocInfo.sType = VK_STRUCTURE_TYPE_COMMAND_BUFFER_ALLOCATE_INF

allocInfo.commandPool = commandPool;

allocInfo.level = VK_COMMAND_BUFFER_LEVEL_PRIMARY;

allocInfo.commandBufferCount = 1;

VkCommandBuffer commandBuffer;

vkAllocateCommandBuffers(device, &allocInfo, &commandBuffer);
```

These steps provide a solid foundation for understanding Vulkan's core concepts. Mastering them is key to leveraging Vulkan's full potential in real-world applications.

Command Buffers and Queues

IN VULKAN, COMMAND buffers and queues are essential components that facilitate the execution of operations on the GPU. Unlike older APIs like OpenGL, where drawing commands are sent directly to the GPU, Vulkan uses an indirect approach where commands are recorded into command buffers and then submitted to queues for execution. This allows developers to batch operations, minimize driver overhead, and better utilize multi-threading capabilities.

Understanding how command buffers and queues work is critical for building efficient Vulkan applications. This section covers the concepts, types, creation, recording, and submission of command buffers and provides a detailed explanation of queues and synchronization mechanisms.

Overview of Command Buffers

A COMMAND BUFFER IN Vulkan is an object that stores a sequence of GPU commands. These commands can include drawing operations, memory transfers, and pipeline state changes. Command buffers are recorded once and can be submitted multiple times, allowing for efficient reuse of recorded commands.

Key characteristics of command buffers:

1. **Explicit Recording**: All commands must be explicitly recorded before execution.
2. **Batch Execution**: Commands are grouped and executed together, reducing driver overhead.
3. **Reusable**: Command buffers can be recorded once and submitted multiple times if the commands do not change.
4. **Thread-Safe Recording**: Multiple threads can record command buffers simultaneously.

Types of Command Buffers

VULKAN PROVIDES TWO levels of command buffers:

1. **Primary Command Buffers**: These can be directly submitted to queues. They contain the main sequence of commands for rendering or compute operations.
2. **Secondary Command Buffers**: These are intended to be

executed within primary command buffers. They are useful for breaking complex operations into smaller, reusable pieces, especially when multi-threading is employed.

Creating a Command Pool

BEFORE CREATING COMMAND buffers, you need a **command pool**. The command pool manages the memory for storing command buffers and provides a mechanism for allocating and freeing them.

Here's an example of how to create a command pool:

```
VkCommandPoolCreateInfo poolInfo = {};

poolInfo.sType = VK_STRUCTURE_TYPE_COMMAND_POOL_CREATE_INFO;

poolInfo.queueFamilyIndex = graphicsQueueFamilyIndex;

poolInfo.flags = VK_COMMAND_POOL_CREATE_RESET_COMMAND_BUFFER

VkCommandPool commandPool;

if (vkCreateCommandPool(device, &poolInfo, NULL, &commandPool) != VK_SUCCESS) {

printf("Failed to create command pool!\n");

}
```

In this example:

- **graphicsQueueFamilyIndex** specifies the queue family that will execute the commands.

- **VK_COMMAND_POOL_CREATE_RESET_COMMAND_B** allows command buffers allocated from this pool to be reset individually.

Allocating Command Buffers

ONCE YOU HAVE A COMMAND pool, you can allocate command buffers from it. Here's how to allocate primary command buffers:

VkCommandBufferAllocateInfo allocInfo = {};

allocInfo.sType = VK_STRUCTURE_TYPE_COMMAND_BUFFER_ALLOCATE_I

allocInfo.commandPool = commandPool;

allocInfo.level = VK_COMMAND_BUFFER_LEVEL_PRIMARY;

allocInfo.commandBufferCount = 1;

VkCommandBuffer commandBuffer;

if (vkAllocateCommandBuffers(device, &allocInfo, &commandBuffer) != VK_SUCCESS) {

printf("Failed to allocate command buffer!\n");

}

In this snippet:

- **commandPool** is the pool from which the command buffer is allocated.

- **VK_COMMAND_BUFFER_LEVEL_PRIMARY** indicates that we are allocating a primary command buffer.

Recording Command Buffers

RECORDING COMMANDS into a command buffer involves starting a recording session, issuing commands, and ending the recording. The recorded commands are stored in the command buffer and can be submitted to a queue later.

Here's a basic example of recording commands into a command buffer:

```
VkCommandBufferBeginInfo beginInfo = {};

beginInfo.sType =
VK_STRUCTURE_TYPE_COMMAND_BUFFER_BEGIN_INFO;

beginInfo.flags =
VK_COMMAND_BUFFER_USAGE_SIMULTANEOUS_USE_BIT;

if (vkBeginCommandBuffer(commandBuffer, &beginInfo) !=
VK_SUCCESS) {

printf("Failed to begin recording command buffer!\n");

}

// Example: clear color

VkClearValue clearColor = {{{0.0f, 0.0f, 0.0f, 1.0f}}};

VkRenderPassBeginInfo renderPassInfo = {};
```

```
renderPassInfo.sType =
VK_STRUCTURE_TYPE_RENDER_PASS_BEGIN_INFO;

renderPassInfo.renderPass = renderPass;

renderPassInfo.framebuffer = framebuffer;

renderPassInfo.renderArea.offset = (VkOffset2D){0, 0};

renderPassInfo.renderArea.extent = swapchainExtent;

renderPassInfo.clearValueCount = 1;

renderPassInfo.pClearValues = &clearColor;

vkCmdBeginRenderPass(commandBuffer, &renderPassInfo,
VK_SUBPASS_CONTENTS_INLINE);

// Draw commands go here...

vkCmdEndRenderPass(commandBuffer);

if (vkEndCommandBuffer(commandBuffer) != VK_SUCCESS) {

printf("Failed to record command buffer!\n");

}
```

Key points in this example:

1. **vkBeginCommandBuffer** starts the recording process.
2. **vkCmdBeginRenderPass** begins a render pass with a specified clear color.
3. **vkCmdEndRenderPass** ends the render pass.
4. **vkEndCommandBuffer** finalizes the recording.

The
VK_COMMAND_BUFFER_USAGE_SIMULTANEOUS_USE_BIT

flag allows the command buffer to be submitted multiple times before it finishes executing.

Submitting Command Buffers to a Queue

AFTER RECORDING A COMMAND buffer, you need to submit it to a queue for execution. Here's how to submit a command buffer to a graphics queue:

```
VkSubmitInfo submitInfo = {};

submitInfo.sType = VK_STRUCTURE_TYPE_SUBMIT_INFO;

submitInfo.commandBufferCount = 1;

submitInfo.pCommandBuffers = &commandBuffer;

VkFenceCreateInfo fenceInfo = {};

fenceInfo.sType = VK_STRUCTURE_TYPE_FENCE_CREATE_INFO;

VkFence fence;

vkCreateFence(device, &fenceInfo, NULL, &fence);

if (vkQueueSubmit(graphicsQueue, 1, &submitInfo, fence) != VK_SUCCESS) {

printf("Failed to submit command buffer to the queue!\n");

}

vkWaitForFences(device, 1, &fence, VK_TRUE, UINT64_MAX);

vkDestroyFence(device, fence, NULL);
```

In this code:

- **VkSubmitInfo** describes the command buffers to submit.
- **vkQueueSubmit** submits the command buffer to the specified **graphics queue**.
- **vkWaitForFences** waits for the command buffer execution to complete.

Synchronization in Vulkan

PROPER SYNCHRONIZATION is essential when working with command buffers and queues to ensure that commands execute in the correct order. Vulkan provides several synchronization primitives:

1. **Fences**: Used to synchronize CPU-GPU operations.
2. **Semaphores**: Used to synchronize operations between queues (e.g., graphics and presentation).
3. **Barriers**: Used within command buffers to manage resource transitions.

Example of a Barrier:

VkImageMemoryBarrier barrier = {};

barrier.sType = VK_STRUCTURE_TYPE_IMAGE_MEMORY_BARRIER;

barrier.oldLayout = VK_IMAGE_LAYOUT_UNDEFINED;

```
barrier.newLayout =
VK_IMAGE_LAYOUT_PRESENT_SRC_KHR;

barrier.srcQueueFamilyIndex =
VK_QUEUE_FAMILY_IGNORED;

barrier.dstQueueFamilyIndex =
VK_QUEUE_FAMILY_IGNORED;

barrier.image = swapchainImage;

barrier.subresourceRange.aspectMask =
VK_IMAGE_ASPECT_COLOR_BIT;

barrier.subresourceRange.baseMipLevel = 0;

barrier.subresourceRange.levelCount = 1;

barrier.subresourceRange.baseArrayLayer = 0;

barrier.subresourceRange.layerCount = 1;

barrier.srcAccessMask = 0;

barrier.dstAccessMask =
VK_ACCESS_COLOR_ATTACHMENT_WRITE_BIT;

vkCmdPipelineBarrier(

commandBuffer,

VK_PIPELINE_STAGE_TOP_OF_PIPE_BIT,

VK_PIPELINE_STAGE_COLOR_ATTACHMENT_OUTPUT_BIT,

0,

0, NULL,
```

0, NULL,

1, &barrier

);

This barrier ensures that an image transitions from **undefined** to **presentation** layout before being presented on screen.

Conclusion

UNDERSTANDING HOW TO create, record, and submit command buffers, as well as manage queues and synchronization, is crucial for efficient Vulkan programming. Command buffers allow for explicit control over GPU operations, enabling high-performance graphics rendering and compute tasks. Mastering these concepts ensures that your applications take full advantage of Vulkan's capabilities and achieve optimal performance on modern hardware.

Pipeline Architecture and Stages

IN VULKAN, THE **pipeline** represents a sequence of programmable and fixed-function stages that the GPU executes to produce rendered output. Unlike older graphics APIs like OpenGL, Vulkan requires the pipeline to be created and configured explicitly before execution. This approach gives developers greater control over performance but also increases the complexity of pipeline management.

Understanding Vulkan's pipeline architecture is critical for optimizing rendering workflows, managing resources efficiently, and fully utilizing the capabilities of modern GPUs. This section covers the structure of Vulkan pipelines, the various pipeline stages, and the process of creating and configuring pipelines.

Overview of Vulkan Pipelines

A **pipeline** in Vulkan defines a fixed sequence of operations for processing input data and producing output images. There are two primary types of pipelines in Vulkan:

1. **Graphics Pipeline**: Used for rendering operations (e.g., drawing triangles, lines, and complex geometry). The graphics pipeline consists of multiple stages, including vertex processing, rasterization, and fragment processing.
2. **Compute Pipeline**: Used for executing compute shaders. Unlike the graphics pipeline, the compute pipeline is simpler and consists of a single stage (the compute shader).

In this section, we will focus primarily on the **graphics pipeline**, as it is the backbone of most rendering operations in Vulkan.

Stages of the Graphics Pipeline

THE GRAPHICS PIPELINE consists of several programmable and fixed-function stages. The stages are executed sequentially, and each stage processes the output of the previous stage.

1. **Input Assembly (IA) Stage**
2. **Vertex Shader (VS) Stage**
3. **Tessellation Control and Evaluation (TCS and TES) Stages** *(optional)*
4. **Geometry Shader (GS) Stage** *(optional)*
5. **Rasterization Stage**
6. **Fragment Shader (FS) Stage**

7. **Color Blending Stage**

Each of these stages plays a specific role in the rendering process.

1. Input Assembly (IA) Stage

THE **Input Assembly** stage is responsible for taking vertex data and assembling it into geometric primitives such as points, lines, or triangles. The input to this stage is provided by **vertex buffers.**

Key Configurations for the IA Stage:

- **Vertex Input Bindings**: Describe the format and stride of vertex data.
- **Vertex Input Attributes**: Define how vertex data maps to shader inputs.
- **Primitive Topology**: Specifies the type of primitives (e.g., VK_PRIMITIVE_TOPOLOGY_TRIANGLE_LIST).

Example of Input Assembly Configuration:

```
VkPipelineVertexInputStateCreateInfo vertexInputInfo = {};

vertexInputInfo.sType = VK_STRUCTURE_TYPE_PIPELINE_VERTEX_INPUT_STATE_C

vertexInputInfo.vertexBindingDescriptionCount = 1;

vertexInputInfo.pVertexBindingDescriptions = &bindingDescription;

vertexInputInfo.vertexAttributeDescriptionCount = 2;
```

```
vertexInputInfo.pVertexAttributeDescriptions =
attributeDescriptions;

VkPipelineInputAssemblyStateCreateInfo inputAssembly = {};

inputAssembly.sType =
VK_STRUCTURE_TYPE_PIPELINE_INPUT_ASSEMBLY_STATE_

inputAssembly.topology =
VK_PRIMITIVE_TOPOLOGY_TRIANGLE_LIST;

inputAssembly.primitiveRestartEnable = VK_FALSE;
```

2. Vertex Shader (VS) Stage

THE **Vertex Shader** stage processes each vertex individually. It applies transformations to vertex positions and calculates per-vertex attributes such as color, texture coordinates, and normals.

Example of a Vertex Shader in GLSL:

```
#version 450

layout(location = 0) in vec2 inPosition;

layout(location = 1) in vec3 inColor;

layout(location = 0) out vec3 fragColor;

void main() {

gl_Position = vec4(inPosition, 0.0, 1.0);

fragColor = inColor;

}
```

In Vulkan, vertex shaders are compiled into **SPIR-V** format before being included in the pipeline.

---

3. Tessellation Control and Evaluation Stages (Optional)

TESSELLATION STAGES are optional and are used to subdivide primitives into smaller segments. This is useful for adding geometric detail to surfaces.

- **Tessellation Control Shader (TCS)**: Determines how primitives are subdivided.
- **Tessellation Evaluation Shader (TES)**: Computes the final vertex positions after tessellation.

---

4. Geometry Shader (GS) Stage (Optional)

THE **Geometry Shader** stage processes entire primitives (points, lines, or triangles). It can generate new primitives or modify existing ones. This stage is optional and is less commonly used due to performance considerations.

---

5. Rasterization Stage

THE **Rasterization** stage converts primitives into fragments, which correspond to pixels on the screen. This stage also performs operations like clipping and culling.

Key Configurations for Rasterization:

- **Polygon Mode**: Specifies how primitives are rendered (e.g., filled, wireframe, or points).

- **Culling Mode**: Determines which faces (front, back, or none) are discarded.

- **Depth Bias**: Offsets the depth values of fragments to prevent artifacts.

Example of Rasterization Configuration:

```
VkPipelineRasterizationStateCreateInfo rasterizer = {};

rasterizer.sType = VK_STRUCTURE_TYPE_PIPELINE_RASTERIZATION_STATE_C

rasterizer.depthClampEnable = VK_FALSE;

rasterizer.rasterizerDiscardEnable = VK_FALSE;

rasterizer.polygonMode = VK_POLYGON_MODE_FILL;

rasterizer.cullMode = VK_CULL_MODE_BACK_BIT;

rasterizer.frontFace = VK_FRONT_FACE_CLOCKWISE;

rasterizer.depthBiasEnable = VK_FALSE;

rasterizer.lineWidth = 1.0f;
```

6. Fragment Shader (FS) Stage

THE **Fragment Shader** stage processes each fragment produced by the rasterization stage. It determines the final color and depth of each pixel.

Example of a Fragment Shader in GLSL:

```
#version 450

layout(location = 0) in vec3 fragColor;
```

```
layout(location = 0) out vec4 outColor;

void main() {

outColor = vec4(fragColor, 1.0);

}
```

7. Color Blending Stage

THE **Color Blending** stage combines the output of the fragment shader with the existing contents of the framebuffer. It can perform operations like alpha blending.

Example of Color Blending Configuration:

```
VkPipelineColorBlendAttachmentState colorBlendAttachment = {};

colorBlendAttachment.colorWriteMask = VK_COLOR_COMPONENT_R_BIT | VK_COLOR_COMPONENT_G_BIT |

VK_COLOR_COMPONENT_B_BIT | VK_COLOR_COMPONENT_A_BIT;

colorBlendAttachment.blendEnable = VK_TRUE;

colorBlendAttachment.srcColorBlendFactor = VK_BLEND_FACTOR_SRC_ALPHA;

colorBlendAttachment.dstColorBlendFactor = VK_BLEND_FACTOR_ONE_MINUS_SRC_ALPHA;

colorBlendAttachment.colorBlendOp = VK_BLEND_OP_ADD;

VkPipelineColorBlendStateCreateInfo colorBlending = {};
```

```
colorBlending.sType =
VK_STRUCTURE_TYPE_PIPELINE_COLOR_BLEND_STATE_CI

colorBlending.logicOpEnable = VK_FALSE;

colorBlending.attachmentCount = 1;

colorBlending.pAttachments = &colorBlendAttachment;
```

Creating the Graphics Pipeline

TO CREATE A GRAPHICS pipeline in Vulkan, you combine all the stage configurations and specify them in a VkGraphicsPipelineCreateInfo structure.

Example of Graphics Pipeline Creation:

```
VkGraphicsPipelineCreateInfo pipelineInfo = {};

pipelineInfo.sType =
VK_STRUCTURE_TYPE_GRAPHICS_PIPELINE_CREATE_INFO

pipelineInfo.stageCount = 2;

pipelineInfo.pStages = shaderStages;

pipelineInfo.pVertexInputState = &vertexInputInfo;

pipelineInfo.pInputAssemblyState = &inputAssembly;

pipelineInfo.pRasterizationState = &rasterizer;

pipelineInfo.pColorBlendState = &colorBlending;

pipelineInfo.layout = pipelineLayout;

pipelineInfo.renderPass = renderPass;
```

```
pipelineInfo.subpass = 0;

VkPipeline graphicsPipeline;

if (vkCreateGraphicsPipelines(device, VK_NULL_HANDLE, 1,
&pipelineInfo, NULL, &graphicsPipeline) != VK_SUCCESS) {

printf("Failed to create graphics pipeline!\n");

}
```

Conclusion

VULKAN'S PIPELINE ARCHITECTURE provides fine-grained control over rendering operations, allowing developers to optimize performance and tailor the pipeline to their application's needs. By understanding the various pipeline stages and their configurations, you can build efficient and powerful graphics applications. Mastery of pipeline creation is essential for leveraging the full potential of Vulkan in real-world scenarios.

Chapter 4: Managing Vulkan Resources

Memory Management in Vulkan

MEMORY MANAGEMENT IN Vulkan is one of the core elements of the API, providing developers with a high degree of control over how resources are allocated and managed. This control comes with the cost of additional complexity, requiring developers to explicitly manage device memory and ensure efficient allocation strategies. Unlike older graphics APIs like OpenGL, which abstracted away many memory management details, Vulkan requires direct interaction with GPU memory. This section covers key concepts, allocation strategies, and best practices for memory management in Vulkan.

Memory Types in Vulkan

VULKAN EXPOSES DIFFERENT types of memory through a system of **memory heaps** and **memory types**. These concepts are critical for understanding how to allocate memory for buffers, images, and other resources.

- **Memory Heaps**: Represent the physical memory resources available on a GPU, such as device-local memory or host-visible memory.

- **Memory Types**: Specify the properties of memory heaps. Each heap can have multiple types, each with different capabilities and constraints.

You can query available memory heaps and types using the VkPhysicalDeviceMemoryProperties structure. Here's an example:

```
VkPhysicalDeviceMemoryProperties memoryProperties;

vkGetPhysicalDeviceMemoryProperties(physicalDevice,
&memoryProperties);

for (uint32_t i = 0; i < memoryProperties.memoryHeapCount;
i++) {

printf("Heap %d: Size = %llu\n", i,
memoryProperties.memoryHeaps[i].size);

}

for (uint32_t i = 0; i < memoryProperties.memoryTypeCount; i++)
{

printf("Memory Type %d: Heap Index = %d, Property Flags = %d\
n",

i, memoryProperties.memoryTypes[i].heapIndex,

memoryProperties.memoryTypes[i].propertyFlags);

}
```

The key property flags for memory types include:

- **VK_MEMORY_PROPERTY_DEVICE_LOCAL_BIT**: Memory that resides on the GPU and offers the best performance for rendering.
- **VK_MEMORY_PROPERTY_HOST_VISIBLE_BIT**: Memory that the CPU can map for data transfers.

- **VK_MEMORY_PROPERTY_HOST_COHERENT_BIT**: Memory that ensures consistency between CPU writes and GPU reads without needing to flush caches.

- **VK_MEMORY_PROPERTY_HOST_CACHED_BIT**: Memory that is cached on the host side, improving read performance.

- **VK_MEMORY_PROPERTY_LAZILY_ALLOCATED_BIT**: Memory for resources like transient attachments that don't require full allocation until needed.

Allocating and Binding Memory

WHEN CREATING BUFFERS or images in Vulkan, you first create the resource and then allocate and bind memory to it. The steps are as follows:

1. **Create the Buffer or Image**: Use vkCreateBuffer or vkCreateImage to create the resource.
2. **Query Memory Requirements**: Call vkGetBufferMemoryRequirements or vkGetImageMemoryRequirements to determine the memory size and alignment.
3. **Allocate Memory**: Use vkAllocateMemory to allocate memory from a suitable memory type.
4. **Bind Memory**: Bind the allocated memory to the buffer or image using vkBindBufferMemory or vkBindImageMemory.

Here's an example of creating a buffer and allocating memory for it:

```
// Step 1: Create a buffer

VkBufferCreateInfo bufferInfo = {};

bufferInfo.sType =
VK_STRUCTURE_TYPE_BUFFER_CREATE_INFO;

bufferInfo.size = 1024; // Buffer size in bytes

bufferInfo.usage =
VK_BUFFER_USAGE_VERTEX_BUFFER_BIT;

bufferInfo.sharingMode =
VK_SHARING_MODE_EXCLUSIVE;

VkBuffer buffer;

vkCreateBuffer(device, &bufferInfo, nullptr, &buffer);

// Step 2: Query memory requirements

VkMemoryRequirements memRequirements;

vkGetBufferMemoryRequirements(device, buffer,
&memRequirements);

// Step 3: Allocate memory

VkMemoryAllocateInfo allocInfo = {};

allocInfo.sType =
VK_STRUCTURE_TYPE_MEMORY_ALLOCATE_INFO;

allocInfo.allocationSize = memRequirements.size;

allocInfo.memoryTypeIndex =
FindMemoryType(memRequirements.memoryTypeBits,
```

```
VK_MEMORY_PROPERTY_HOST_VISIBLE_BIT |

VK_MEMORY_PROPERTY_HOST_COHERENT_BIT);

VkDeviceMemory bufferMemory;

vkAllocateMemory(device, &allocInfo, nullptr, &bufferMemory);

// Step 4: Bind memory to buffer

vkBindBufferMemory(device, buffer, bufferMemory, 0);
```

The FindMemoryType function helps you select an appropriate memory type based on requirements:

```
uint32_t FindMemoryType(uint32_t typeFilter, VkMemoryPropertyFlags properties) {

for (uint32_t i = 0; i < memoryProperties.memoryTypeCount; i++) {

if ((typeFilter & (1 << i)) &&

(memoryProperties.memoryTypes[i].propertyFlags & properties) == properties) {

return i;

}

}

throw std::runtime_error("Failed to find suitable memory type!");

}
```

Memory Mapping and Data Transfers

FOR DATA UPLOADS TO the GPU, such as vertex or uniform data, you often need to map memory so the CPU can write to it. Memory mapping involves making a region of GPU memory accessible to the CPU.

Here's an example of mapping memory and copying data to a buffer:

```
void* data;

vkMapMemory(device, bufferMemory, 0, bufferSize, 0, &data);

memcpy(data, vertices.data(), (size_t)bufferSize);

vkUnmapMemory(device, bufferMemory);
```

Key Considerations:

- **vkMapMemory**: Maps the memory to a host-accessible pointer.
- **vkUnmapMemory**: Unmaps the memory after data transfer. Changes are flushed to the GPU if the memory is not HOST_COHERENT.

If the memory is not host-coherent, you need to explicitly flush the mapped range using vkFlushMappedMemoryRanges:

```
VkMappedMemoryRange mappedRange = {};

mappedRange.sType = VK_STRUCTURE_TYPE_MAPPED_MEMORY_RANGE;

mappedRange.memory = bufferMemory;

mappedRange.offset = 0;
```

mappedRange.size = bufferSize;

vkFlushMappedMemoryRanges(device, 1, &mappedRange);

Efficient Memory Allocation Strategies

EFFICIENT MEMORY ALLOCATION is critical for performance. Vulkan provides flexibility in how you allocate memory, but this comes with responsibility for optimization. Key strategies include:

1. **Batch Allocations**: Instead of allocating memory for each resource separately, allocate a large block of memory and suballocate regions for multiple resources.
2. **Alignment Constraints**: Ensure that offsets respect the alignment constraints specified by VkMemoryRequirements::alignment.
3. **Memory Pools**: Use memory pools to manage memory for transient objects, such as command buffers or framebuffers, to reduce fragmentation.
4. **Dedicated Allocations**: For large resources, consider using dedicated allocations rather than suballocating from a pool. Vulkan offers VK_KHR_dedicated_allocation for this purpose.

Releasing Memory

WHEN YOU NO LONGER need resources, it's essential to free the associated memory to avoid leaks. Free buffers and memory with:

vkDestroyBuffer(device, buffer, nullptr);

vkFreeMemory(device, bufferMemory, nullptr);

Best Practices for Memory Management

- **Minimize Allocations**: Frequent memory allocations and deallocations can lead to fragmentation. Allocate in bulk when possible.

- **Reuse Memory**: Reuse memory for similar resources across frames.

- **Defragmentation**: Consider defragmenting memory for long-running applications.

- **GPU-CPU Synchronization**: Avoid stalls by ensuring efficient synchronization between GPU and CPU memory accesses.

Summary

MEMORY MANAGEMENT IN Vulkan offers great control and flexibility but requires careful handling. By understanding memory heaps, types, allocation, and mapping strategies, you can optimize resource management for high-performance graphics applications. Effective use of batch allocations, memory pools, and synchronization primitives will help you achieve efficient and scalable memory usage.

Buffers and Images

BUFFERS AND IMAGES are essential components in Vulkan for managing data, whether it's vertex data, uniform data, or texture data. Understanding how to create, manage, and use buffers and images effectively is crucial for building efficient and performant Vulkan applications. This section explores buffers and images in detail, covering their creation, types, memory requirements, and usage patterns.

Buffers in Vulkan

IN VULKAN, BUFFERS are linear arrays of memory used to store various types of data, such as vertices, indices, or uniform values. Buffers can be created for different purposes, and their usage depends on the type of data they hold.

Creating Buffers

BUFFERS ARE CREATED with the vkCreateBuffer function. The VkBufferCreateInfo structure specifies details such as buffer size, usage flags, and sharing mode. Here's a basic example of creating a buffer for vertex data:

```
VkBufferCreateInfo bufferCreateInfo = {};

bufferCreateInfo.sType = VK_STRUCTURE_TYPE_BUFFER_CREATE_INFO;

bufferCreateInfo.size = sizeof(vertices); // Size of the buffer

bufferCreateInfo.usage = VK_BUFFER_USAGE_VERTEX_BUFFER_BIT;

bufferCreateInfo.sharingMode = VK_SHARING_MODE_EXCLUSIVE;

VkBuffer vertexBuffer;

VkResult result = vkCreateBuffer(device, &bufferCreateInfo, nullptr, &vertexBuffer);

if (result != VK_SUCCESS) {
```

```
throw std::runtime_error("Failed to create vertex buffer!");
}
```

Buffer Usage Flags

WHEN CREATING A BUFFER, you specify its intended use with VkBufferUsageFlags. Some common usage flags include:

- **VK_BUFFER_USAGE_VERTEX_BUFFER_BIT**: For vertex data.
- **VK_BUFFER_USAGE_INDEX_BUFFER_BIT**: For index data.
- **VK_BUFFER_USAGE_UNIFORM_BUFFER_BIT**: For uniform buffer data.
- **VK_BUFFER_USAGE_STORAGE_BUFFER_BIT**: For general-purpose storage buffers.
- **VK_BUFFER_USAGE_TRANSFER_SRC_BIT**: For buffers that will be used as a source in a transfer operation.
- **VK_BUFFER_USAGE_TRANSFER_DST_BIT**: For buffers that will be used as a destination in a transfer operation.

You can combine multiple flags using the bitwise OR operator. For example:

bufferCreateInfo.usage = VK_BUFFER_USAGE_VERTEX_BUFFER_BIT | VK_BUFFER_USAGE_TRANSFER_DST_BIT;

Querying Buffer Memory Requirements

AFTER CREATING A BUFFER, you need to allocate memory for it. Use vkGetBufferMemoryRequirements to determine the size, alignment, and memory type requirements:

VkMemoryRequirements memRequirements;

vkGetBufferMemoryRequirements(device, vertexBuffer, &memRequirements);

std::cout << "Memory size: " << memRequirements.size << std::endl;

std::cout << "Alignment: " << memRequirements.alignment << std::endl;

std::cout << "Memory type bits: " << memRequirements.memoryTypeBits << std::endl;

Binding Memory to Buffers

AFTER ALLOCATING MEMORY, bind it to the buffer using vkBindBufferMemory:

VkDeviceMemory bufferMemory;

VkMemoryAllocateInfo allocInfo = {};

allocInfo.sType = VK_STRUCTURE_TYPE_MEMORY_ALLOCATE_INFO;

```
allocInfo.allocationSize = memRequirements.size;

allocInfo.memoryTypeIndex =
FindMemoryType(memRequirements.memoryTypeBits,
VK_MEMORY_PROPERTY_HOST_VISIBLE_BIT |
VK_MEMORY_PROPERTY_HOST_COHERENT_BIT);

vkAllocateMemory(device, &allocInfo, nullptr, &bufferMemory);

vkBindBufferMemory(device, vertexBuffer, bufferMemory, 0);
```

Mapping Buffers to Host Memory

TO UPDATE BUFFER DATA from the CPU, map the memory and write to it:

```
void* data;

vkMapMemory(device, bufferMemory, 0, bufferSize, 0, &data);

memcpy(data, vertices.data(), (size_t)bufferSize);

vkUnmapMemory(device, bufferMemory);
```

If the memory type is not host-coherent, you need to flush the mapped memory:

```
VkMappedMemoryRange mappedRange = {};

mappedRange.sType =
VK_STRUCTURE_TYPE_MAPPED_MEMORY_RANGE;

mappedRange.memory = bufferMemory;

mappedRange.offset = 0;

mappedRange.size = bufferSize;
```

vkFlushMappedMemoryRanges(device, 1, &mappedRange);

Types of Buffers

BUFFERS IN VULKAN CAN be used for different purposes:

1. **Vertex Buffers**: Store vertex data such as positions, normals, and texture coordinates.
2. **Index Buffers**: Store indices for indexed drawing, reducing data redundancy.
3. **Uniform Buffers**: Store uniform data shared across shaders.
4. **Storage Buffers**: General-purpose buffers accessible in compute and fragment shaders.
5. **Staging Buffers**: Temporary buffers for data transfers.

Images in Vulkan

IMAGES IN VULKAN REPRESENT multidimensional data such as textures or framebuffers. Images are more complex than buffers due to their various formats, dimensions, and usage patterns.

Creating Images

IMAGES ARE CREATED with the vkCreateImage function. The VkImageCreateInfo structure defines the image properties:

VkImageCreateInfo imageCreateInfo = {};

imageCreateInfo.sType = VK_STRUCTURE_TYPE_IMAGE_CREATE_INFO;

imageCreateInfo.imageType = VK_IMAGE_TYPE_2D;

imageCreateInfo.extent.width = 512;

```
imageCreateInfo.extent.height = 512;

imageCreateInfo.extent.depth = 1;

imageCreateInfo.mipLevels = 1;

imageCreateInfo.arrayLayers = 1;

imageCreateInfo.format = VK_FORMAT_R8G8B8A8_SRGB;

imageCreateInfo.tiling = VK_IMAGE_TILING_OPTIMAL;

imageCreateInfo.initialLayout =
VK_IMAGE_LAYOUT_UNDEFINED;

imageCreateInfo.usage =
VK_IMAGE_USAGE_TRANSFER_DST_BIT |
VK_IMAGE_USAGE_SAMPLED_BIT;

imageCreateInfo.samples = VK_SAMPLE_COUNT_1_BIT;

imageCreateInfo.sharingMode =
VK_SHARING_MODE_EXCLUSIVE;

VkImage textureImage;

if (vkCreateImage(device, &imageCreateInfo, nullptr,
&textureImage) != VK_SUCCESS) {

throw std::runtime_error("Failed to create image!");

}
```

Image Types

THE IMAGETYPE FIELD defines the dimensionality of the image:

- **VK_IMAGE_TYPE_1D**: For 1D textures.
- **VK_IMAGE_TYPE_2D**: For 2D textures and render targets.
- **VK_IMAGE_TYPE_3D**: For 3D textures.

Image Formats

THE FORMAT FIELD SPECIFIES the data format, such as:

- **VK_FORMAT_R8G8B8A8_UNORM**: 8-bit unsigned normalized RGBA.
- **VK_FORMAT_D32_SFLOAT**: 32-bit float depth format.

Image Usage Flags

COMMON IMAGE USAGE flags include:

- **VK_IMAGE_USAGE_TRANSFER_SRC_BIT**: For images used as a transfer source.
- **VK_IMAGE_USAGE_TRANSFER_DST_BIT**: For images used as a transfer destination.
- **VK_IMAGE_USAGE_SAMPLED_BIT**: For images sampled in shaders.
- **VK_IMAGE_USAGE_COLOR_ATTACHMENT_BIT**: For render target attachments.

- VK_IMAGE_USAGE_DEPTH_STENCIL_ATTACHMENT_ For depth/stencil attachments.

Allocating and Binding Memory to Images

ALLOCATE AND BIND MEMORY to images similarly to buffers:

VkMemoryRequirements memRequirements;

vkGetImageMemoryRequirements(device, textureImage, &memRequirements);

VkMemoryAllocateInfo allocInfo = {};

allocInfo.sType = VK_STRUCTURE_TYPE_MEMORY_ALLOCATE_INFO;

allocInfo.allocationSize = memRequirements.size;

allocInfo.memoryTypeIndex = FindMemoryType(memRequirements.memoryTypeBits, VK_MEMORY_PROPERTY_DEVICE_LOCAL_BIT);

VkDeviceMemory textureImageMemory;

vkAllocateMemory(device, &allocInfo, nullptr, &textureImageMemory);

vkBindImageMemory(device, textureImage, textureImageMemory, 0);

Image Views

TO USE AN IMAGE IN shaders or framebuffers, create an image view:

```
VkImageViewCreateInfo viewInfo = {};

viewInfo.sType = VK_STRUCTURE_TYPE_IMAGE_VIEW_CREATE_INFO;

viewInfo.image = textureImage;

viewInfo.viewType = VK_IMAGE_VIEW_TYPE_2D;

viewInfo.format = VK_FORMAT_R8G8B8A8_SRGB;

viewInfo.subresourceRange.aspectMask = VK_IMAGE_ASPECT_COLOR_BIT;

viewInfo.subresourceRange.baseMipLevel = 0;

viewInfo.subresourceRange.levelCount = 1;

viewInfo.subresourceRange.baseArrayLayer = 0;

viewInfo.subresourceRange.layerCount = 1;

VkImageView textureImageView;

if (vkCreateImageView(device, &viewInfo, nullptr, &textureImageView) != VK_SUCCESS) {

throw std::runtime_error("Failed to create texture image view!");

}
```

Summary

BUFFERS AND IMAGES form the foundation of data management in Vulkan. Buffers handle linear data like vertices and indices, while images manage multidimensional data like textures. Understanding how to create, allocate, and bind memory for these resources is essential for developing efficient Vulkan applications. Effective use of usage flags, memory mapping, and synchronization ensures optimal performance and flexibility.

Descriptor Sets and Pools

DESCRIPTORS IN VULKAN are a mechanism that allows shaders to access resources such as buffers, images, and samplers. They provide a flexible and powerful way to manage data passed to the GPU. Descriptor sets, layouts, and pools are the key components for managing descriptors, and understanding their structure and lifecycle is essential for efficient resource management in Vulkan.

Overview of Descriptors and Descriptor Sets

DESCRIPTORS DEFINE how resources are bound to shaders. A **descriptor** represents a binding to a resource like a buffer or an image. A **descriptor set** is a collection of descriptors that can be bound to a pipeline for use by shaders. Descriptor sets are created from a **descriptor set layout**, which defines the types of resources that will be bound and their binding points.

For example, if a shader needs a uniform buffer and a texture, the descriptor set layout will describe these resources, and the descriptor set will provide the actual buffer and texture bindings.

Descriptor Set Layouts

A DESCRIPTOR SET LAYOUT specifies the types and number of descriptors that will be used. To create a descriptor set layout, use the VkDescriptorSetLayoutCreateInfo structure. Here's an example of creating a layout with a uniform buffer and a combined image sampler:

```
VkDescriptorSetLayoutBinding uboLayoutBinding = {};

uboLayoutBinding.binding = 0;

uboLayoutBinding.descriptorType = VK_DESCRIPTOR_TYPE_UNIFORM_BUFFER;

uboLayoutBinding.descriptorCount = 1;

uboLayoutBinding.stageFlags = VK_SHADER_STAGE_VERTEX_BIT;

uboLayoutBinding.pImmutableSamplers = nullptr;

VkDescriptorSetLayoutBinding samplerLayoutBinding = {};

samplerLayoutBinding.binding = 1;

samplerLayoutBinding.descriptorType = VK_DESCRIPTOR_TYPE_COMBINED_IMAGE_SAMPLER;

samplerLayoutBinding.descriptorCount = 1;

samplerLayoutBinding.stageFlags = VK_SHADER_STAGE_FRAGMENT_BIT;

samplerLayoutBinding.pImmutableSamplers = nullptr;

std::array<VkDescriptorSetLayoutBinding, 2> bindings = {uboLayoutBinding, samplerLayoutBinding};
```

```
VkDescriptorSetLayoutCreateInfo layoutInfo = {};

layoutInfo.sType =
VK_STRUCTURE_TYPE_DESCRIPTOR_SET_LAYOUT_CREAT

layoutInfo.bindingCount = static_cast<uint32_t>(bindings.size());

layoutInfo.pBindings = bindings.data();

VkDescriptorSetLayout descriptorSetLayout;

if (vkCreateDescriptorSetLayout(device, &layoutInfo, nullptr,
&descriptorSetLayout) != VK_SUCCESS) {

throw std::runtime_error("Failed to create descriptor set layout!");

}
```

Descriptor Pools

DESCRIPTOR POOLS MANAGE the memory for descriptor sets. A descriptor pool allows you to allocate multiple descriptor sets of different types efficiently. When creating a descriptor pool, you specify the maximum number of descriptors of each type that the pool can allocate.

Here's an example of creating a descriptor pool for uniform buffers and combined image samplers:

```
std::array<VkDescriptorPoolSize, 2> poolSizes = {};

poolSizes[0].type =
VK_DESCRIPTOR_TYPE_UNIFORM_BUFFER;

poolSizes[0].descriptorCount = 10;
```

```
poolSizes[1].type = VK_DESCRIPTOR_TYPE_COMBINED_IMAGE_SAMPLER;

poolSizes[1].descriptorCount = 10;

VkDescriptorPoolCreateInfo poolInfo = {};

poolInfo.sType = VK_STRUCTURE_TYPE_DESCRIPTOR_POOL_CREATE_INFO;

poolInfo.poolSizeCount = static_cast<uint32_t>(poolSizes.size());

poolInfo.pPoolSizes = poolSizes.data();

poolInfo.maxSets = 10;

VkDescriptorPool descriptorPool;

if (vkCreateDescriptorPool(device, &poolInfo, nullptr, &descriptorPool) != VK_SUCCESS) {

throw std::runtime_error("Failed to create descriptor pool!");

}
```

Allocating Descriptor Sets

DESCRIPTOR SETS ARE allocated from descriptor pools using the vkAllocateDescriptorSets function. You need to specify the descriptor set layout that the allocated descriptor sets will conform to.

Here's an example of allocating a descriptor set:

```
VkDescriptorSetAllocateInfo allocInfo = {};

allocInfo.sType = VK_STRUCTURE_TYPE_DESCRIPTOR_SET_ALLOCATE_INFO;
```

```
allocInfo.descriptorPool = descriptorPool;

allocInfo.descriptorSetCount = 1;

allocInfo.pSetLayouts = &descriptorSetLayout;

VkDescriptorSet descriptorSet;

if (vkAllocateDescriptorSets(device, &allocInfo, &descriptorSet) != VK_SUCCESS) {

throw std::runtime_error("Failed to allocate descriptor set!");

}
```

Updating Descriptor Sets

ONCE A DESCRIPTOR SET is allocated, you need to update it with the actual resources (buffers or images) that it references. This is done using the vkUpdateDescriptorSets function.

Example: Updating a Uniform Buffer Descriptor

HERE'S AN EXAMPLE OF updating a descriptor set with a uniform buffer:

```
VkDescriptorBufferInfo bufferInfo = {};

bufferInfo.buffer = uniformBuffer;

bufferInfo.offset = 0;

bufferInfo.range = sizeof(UniformBufferObject);

VkWriteDescriptorSet descriptorWrite = {};
```

descriptorWrite.sType = VK_STRUCTURE_TYPE_WRITE_DESCRIPTOR_SET;

descriptorWrite.dstSet = descriptorSet;

descriptorWrite.dstBinding = 0;

descriptorWrite.dstArrayElement = 0;

descriptorWrite.descriptorType = VK_DESCRIPTOR_TYPE_UNIFORM_BUFFER;

descriptorWrite.descriptorCount = 1;

descriptorWrite.pBufferInfo = &bufferInfo;

vkUpdateDescriptorSets(device, 1, &descriptorWrite, 0, nullptr);

Example: Updating a Combined Image Sampler Descriptor

HERE'S HOW TO UPDATE a descriptor set with a combined image sampler:

VkDescriptorImageInfo imageInfo = {};

imageInfo.imageLayout = VK_IMAGE_LAYOUT_SHADER_READ_ONLY_OPTIMAL;

imageInfo.imageView = textureImageView;

imageInfo.sampler = textureSampler;

VkWriteDescriptorSet descriptorWrite = {};

descriptorWrite.sType = VK_STRUCTURE_TYPE_WRITE_DESCRIPTOR_SET;

descriptorWrite.dstSet = descriptorSet;

```
descriptorWrite.dstBinding = 1;

descriptorWrite.dstArrayElement = 0;

descriptorWrite.descriptorType = VK_DESCRIPTOR_TYPE_COMBINED_IMAGE_SAMPLER;

descriptorWrite.descriptorCount = 1;

descriptorWrite.pImageInfo = &imageInfo;

vkUpdateDescriptorSets(device, 1, &descriptorWrite, 0, nullptr);
```

Binding Descriptor Sets

DESCRIPTOR SETS ARE bound to the graphics pipeline before drawing. Use vkCmdBindDescriptorSets to bind descriptor sets:

```
vkCmdBindDescriptorSets(commandBuffer, VK_PIPELINE_BIND_POINT_GRAPHICS, pipelineLayout, 0, 1, &descriptorSet, 0, nullptr);
```

Descriptor Set Lifecycle

MANAGING THE LIFECYCLE of descriptor sets and pools is important for efficient resource usage:

1. **Create Descriptor Set Layout**: Define the layout of descriptors.
2. **Create Descriptor Pool**: Allocate a pool large enough for your descriptor needs.
3. **Allocate Descriptor Sets**: Allocate descriptor sets from the pool.
4. **Update Descriptor Sets**: Populate descriptor sets with actual resources.
5. **Bind Descriptor Sets**: Bind the sets during rendering.

6. **Destroy Resources**: Clean up descriptor sets, pools, and layouts when no longer needed.

Cleaning Up

WHEN YOU'RE DONE WITH descriptor sets and pools, clean them up properly:

vkDestroyDescriptorPool(device, descriptorPool, nullptr);

vkDestroyDescriptorSetLayout(device, descriptorSetLayout, nullptr);

Best Practices for Descriptors

- **Reuse Descriptor Pools**: Instead of creating new pools frequently, reuse existing ones to reduce overhead.

- **Batch Allocations**: Allocate descriptor sets in batches to minimize the number of allocation calls.

- **Descriptor Set Recycling**: Recycle descriptor sets for dynamic resources instead of reallocating them.

- **Use Dynamic Descriptors**: For resources that change frequently, use dynamic uniform buffers to minimize updates.

Summary

DESCRIPTOR SETS AND pools in Vulkan provide a powerful and flexible way to manage resources for shaders. By understanding descriptor set layouts, pools, and the update process, you can efficiently manage buffers, images, and samplers in your applications. Proper allocation, updating, and binding of descriptor sets are critical for achieving optimal performance and flexibility in Vulkan-based rendering.

Chapter 5: Rendering Basics in Vulkan

Creating a Vulkan Swapchain

A SWAPCHAIN IN VULKAN is fundamental for presenting images to a display. It represents a collection of images that can be rendered to and shown on the screen. In this section, we'll explore what a swapchain is, its purpose, and how to create one in Vulkan. This step-by-step approach ensures you understand each component involved, from setting up the presentation surface to integrating the swapchain with the rendering loop.

Understanding the Swapchain

IN VULKAN, THE SWAPCHAIN is a mechanism that manages the images used for presentation. Typically, a swapchain contains multiple images (commonly two or three), and these images are used in a sequence to minimize latency and allow for smoother rendering. This process is often referred to as **double buffering** or **triple buffering**.

- **Double Buffering**: One image is being displayed while the next image is being rendered.

- **Triple Buffering**: Two images are rendered alternately while a third image is displayed.

The swapchain works with a **presentation engine** that interfaces with the operating system's windowing system. The presentation engine handles the actual display of the images, while the swapchain handles the sequence of rendering and presenting.

Steps to Create a Swapchain

TO CREATE A SWAPCHAIN in Vulkan, the following steps are typically followed:

1. **Create a Presentation Surface**
2. **Select a Surface Format**
3. **Choose a Presentation Mode**
4. **Determine the Swapchain Extent**
5. **Create the Swapchain Object**
6. **Retrieve Swapchain Images**
7. **Create Image Views for Swapchain Images**

Let's explore each step in detail with code snippets where necessary.

Step 1: Create a Presentation Surface

THE PRESENTATION SURFACE represents the platform-specific window or display surface where images will be presented. Creating a surface is platform-dependent, but Vulkan abstracts it using the VkSurfaceKHR type.

For example, on **Windows**, you can create a surface like this:

VkWin32SurfaceCreateInfoKHR createInfo = {};

createInfo.sType = VK_STRUCTURE_TYPE_WIN32_SURFACE_CREATE_INFO_K

createInfo.hwnd = hwnd; // Handle to the window

createInfo.hinstance = GetModuleHandle(nullptr);

VkSurfaceKHR surface;

if (vkCreateWin32SurfaceKHR(instance, &createInfo, nullptr, &surface) != VK_SUCCESS) {

throw std::runtime_error("Failed to create window surface!");

}

On **Linux (X11)**, the code would look different:

VkXlibSurfaceCreateInfoKHR createInfo = {};

createInfo.sType = VK_STRUCTURE_TYPE_XLIB_SURFACE_CREATE_INFO_KHR

createInfo.dpy = display; // Pointer to the display

createInfo.window = window; // Window handle

VkSurfaceKHR surface;

if (vkCreateXlibSurfaceKHR(instance, &createInfo, nullptr, &surface) != VK_SUCCESS) {

throw std::runtime_error("Failed to create window surface!");

}

Step 2: Select a Surface Format

THE SURFACE FORMAT determines the color space and the format of the images in the swapchain. Commonly used formats include VK_FORMAT_B8G8R8A8_SRGB and VK_COLOR_SPACE_SRGB_NONLINEAR_KHR.

First, query the available surface formats:

uint32_t formatCount;

```
vkGetPhysicalDeviceSurfaceFormatsKHR(physicalDevice, surface,
&formatCount, nullptr);

std::vector<VkSurfaceFormatKHR> formats(formatCount);

vkGetPhysicalDeviceSurfaceFormatsKHR(physicalDevice, surface,
&formatCount, formats.data());
```

Then, select a suitable format:

```
VkSurfaceFormatKHR chosenFormat = formats[0];

for (const auto& availableFormat : formats) {

if (availableFormat.format == VK_FORMAT_B8G8R8A8_SRGB
&&

availableFormat.colorSpace ==
VK_COLOR_SPACE_SRGB_NONLINEAR_KHR) {

chosenFormat = availableFormat;

break;

}

}
```

Step 3: Choose a Presentation Mode

THE PRESENTATION MODE defines how images are swapped between the application and the presentation engine. Vulkan supports several presentation modes:

- **VK_PRESENT_MODE_FIFO_KHR**: Classic vertical sync (V-Sync).

- **VK_PRESENT_MODE_MAILBOX_KHR**: Triple buffering with the ability to replace queued images.

- **VK_PRESENT_MODE_IMMEDIATE_KHR**: No buffering, images are presented immediately.

Example code to choose a presentation mode:

```
VkPresentModeKHR chosenPresentMode = VK_PRESENT_MODE_FIFO_KHR; // Default mode

for (const auto& availablePresentMode : availablePresentModes) {

if (availablePresentMode == VK_PRESENT_MODE_MAILBOX_KHR) {

chosenPresentMode = VK_PRESENT_MODE_MAILBOX_KHR;

break;

}

}
```

Step 4: Determine the Swapchain Extent

THE SWAPCHAIN EXTENT specifies the resolution of the swapchain images. It is typically set to match the resolution of the window.

Example code to determine the extent:

```
VkSurfaceCapabilitiesKHR capabilities;

vkGetPhysicalDeviceSurfaceCapabilitiesKHR(physicalDevice, surface, &capabilities);
```

```
VkExtent2D extent = capabilities.currentExtent;

if (capabilities.currentExtent.width == UINT32_MAX) {

extent.width = std::clamp(width,
capabilities.minImageExtent.width,
capabilities.maxImageExtent.width);

extent.height = std::clamp(height,
capabilities.minImageExtent.height,
capabilities.maxImageExtent.height);

}
```

Step 5: Create the Swapchain Object

NOW THAT WE HAVE ALL the necessary details, we can create the swapchain:

```
VkSwapchainCreateInfoKHR createInfo = {};

createInfo.sType =
VK_STRUCTURE_TYPE_SWAPCHAIN_CREATE_INFO_KHR;

createInfo.surface = surface;

createInfo.minImageCount = imageCount; // Typically 2 or 3

createInfo.imageFormat = chosenFormat.format;

createInfo.imageColorSpace = chosenFormat.colorSpace;

createInfo.imageExtent = extent;

createInfo.imageArrayLayers = 1;

createInfo.imageUsage =
VK_IMAGE_USAGE_COLOR_ATTACHMENT_BIT;
```

```
VkSwapchainKHR swapchain;

if (vkCreateSwapchainKHR(device, &createInfo, nullptr, &swapchain) != VK_SUCCESS) {

throw std::runtime_error("Failed to create swapchain!");

}
```

Step 6: Retrieve Swapchain Images

ONCE THE SWAPCHAIN is created, retrieve the images associated with it:

```
uint32_t imageCount;

vkGetSwapchainImagesKHR(device, swapchain, &imageCount, nullptr);

std::vector<VkImage> swapchainImages(imageCount);

vkGetSwapchainImagesKHR(device, swapchain, &imageCount, swapchainImages.data());
```

Step 7: Create Image Views for Swapchain Images

FOR EACH SWAPCHAIN image, create an image view to use in the render pipeline:

```
std::vector<VkImageView>
swapchainImageViews(swapchainImages.size());

for (size_t i = 0; i < swapchainImages.size(); i++) {

VkImageViewCreateInfo createInfo = {};
```

```
createInfo.sType = VK_STRUCTURE_TYPE_IMAGE_VIEW_CREATE_INFO;

createInfo.image = swapchainImages[i];

createInfo.viewType = VK_IMAGE_VIEW_TYPE_2D;

createInfo.format = chosenFormat.format;

createInfo.components.r = VK_COMPONENT_SWIZZLE_IDENTITY;

createInfo.components.g = VK_COMPONENT_SWIZZLE_IDENTITY;

createInfo.components.b = VK_COMPONENT_SWIZZLE_IDENTITY;

createInfo.components.a = VK_COMPONENT_SWIZZLE_IDENTITY;

createInfo.subresourceRange.aspectMask = VK_IMAGE_ASPECT_COLOR_BIT;

createInfo.subresourceRange.baseMipLevel = 0;

createInfo.subresourceRange.levelCount = 1;

createInfo.subresourceRange.baseArrayLayer = 0;

createInfo.subresourceRange.layerCount = 1;

if (vkCreateImageView(device, &createInfo, nullptr, &swapchainImageViews[i]) != VK_SUCCESS) {

throw std::runtime_error("Failed to create image views!");

}
```

```
}
```

Conclusion

CREATING A SWAPCHAIN in Vulkan involves multiple steps to ensure the rendering pipeline works smoothly. By understanding these steps, you gain a foundational grasp of how Vulkan handles presentation and rendering to the screen. Once the swapchain is set up, you can proceed to draw your first frame and handle synchronization, which we will cover in the next sections.

Rendering a Triangle

RENDERING A BASIC TRIANGLE is a fundamental step in learning Vulkan. Though Vulkan is more verbose and lower-level than other APIs like OpenGL, drawing a triangle introduces many core concepts such as creating pipelines, allocating buffers, handling shaders, and synchronizing rendering operations. In this section, we'll walk through the complete process required to render a triangle on the screen.

The key stages to rendering a triangle are:

1. **Defining the Vertex Data**
2. **Creating a Vertex Buffer**
3. **Writing Shader Modules**
4. **Creating the Graphics Pipeline**
5. **Recording Command Buffers**
6. **Drawing and Presenting**
7. **Synchronizing Rendering Operations**

Step 1: Defining the Vertex Data

TO DRAW A TRIANGLE, you need to define its vertices. Each vertex will have a position in 2D or 3D space. For simplicity, we'll define a triangle with three vertices in normalized device coordinates (NDC).

```
struct Vertex {

glm::vec2 pos;

glm::vec3 color;

};

const std::vector<Vertex> vertices = {

{{0.0f, -0.5f}, {1.0f, 0.0f, 0.0f}}, // Bottom vertex (red)

{{0.5f, 0.5f}, {0.0f, 1.0f, 0.0f}}, // Right vertex (green)

{{-0.5f, 0.5f}, {0.0f, 0.0f, 1.0f}} // Left vertex (blue)

};
```

This Vertex struct contains position and color attributes. We'll use these attributes in our vertex shader to position the triangle and color it.

Step 2: Creating a Vertex Buffer

TO STORE VERTEX DATA on the GPU, you need a **vertex buffer**. In Vulkan, creating a buffer involves allocating memory and copying data into it.

Create the Vertex Buffer

VKBUFFER VERTEXBUFFER;

VkDeviceMemory vertexBufferMemory;

createBuffer(

sizeof(vertices[0]) * vertices.size(),

VK_BUFFER_USAGE_VERTEX_BUFFER_BIT,

VK_MEMORY_PROPERTY_HOST_VISIBLE_BIT | VK_MEMORY_PROPERTY_HOST_COHERENT_BIT,

vertexBuffer,

vertexBufferMemory

);

The createBuffer function abstracts the details of buffer creation. Here's an implementation for it:

void createBuffer(VkDeviceSize size, VkBufferUsageFlags usage, VkMemoryPropertyFlags properties,

VkBuffer& buffer, VkDeviceMemory& bufferMemory) {

VkBufferCreateInfo bufferInfo = {};

bufferInfo.sType = VK_STRUCTURE_TYPE_BUFFER_CREATE_INFO;

bufferInfo.size = size;

bufferInfo.usage = usage;

```
bufferInfo.sharingMode = VK_SHARING_MODE_EXCLUSIVE;

if (vkCreateBuffer(device, &bufferInfo, nullptr, &buffer) != VK_SUCCESS) {

throw std::runtime_error("Failed to create buffer!");

}

VkMemoryRequirements memRequirements;

vkGetBufferMemoryRequirements(device, buffer, &memRequirements);

VkMemoryAllocateInfo allocInfo = {};

allocInfo.sType = VK_STRUCTURE_TYPE_MEMORY_ALLOCATE_INFO;

allocInfo.allocationSize = memRequirements.size;

allocInfo.memoryTypeIndex = findMemoryType(memRequirements.memoryTypeBits, properties);

if (vkAllocateMemory(device, &allocInfo, nullptr, &bufferMemory) != VK_SUCCESS) {

throw std::runtime_error("Failed to allocate buffer memory!");

}

vkBindBufferMemory(device, buffer, bufferMemory, 0);

}
```

Copy Vertex Data to the Buffer

ONCE THE BUFFER IS created, map it and copy the vertex data:

```
void* data;

vkMapMemory(device, vertexBufferMemory, 0, bufferSize, 0, &data);

memcpy(data, vertices.data(), (size_t)bufferSize);

vkUnmapMemory(device, vertexBufferMemory);
```

Step 3: Writing Shader Modules

VULKAN USES SHADERS written in SPIR-V format. For rendering a triangle, you need at least a vertex shader and a fragment shader.

Vertex Shader (GLSL)

```
#VERSION 450

layout(location = 0) in vec2 inPos;

layout(location = 1) in vec3 inColor;

layout(location = 0) out vec3 fragColor;

void main() {

gl_Position = vec4(inPos, 0.0, 1.0);

fragColor = inColor;

}
```

Fragment Shader (GLSL)

#VERSION 450

layout(location = 0) in vec3 fragColor;

layout(location = 0) out vec4 outColor;

void main() {

outColor = vec4(fragColor, 1.0);

}

Compile these shaders to SPIR-V using glslc:

glslc vertex_shader.vert -o vertex_shader.spv

glslc fragment_shader.frag -o fragment_shader.spv

Load Shader Modules in Code

VKSHADERMODULE VERTEXSHADERMODULE = createShaderModule("vertex_shader.spv");

VkShaderModule fragmentShaderModule = createShaderModule("fragment_shader.spv");

Step 4: Creating the Graphics Pipeline

THE GRAPHICS PIPELINE defines how the drawing commands are processed. To create a pipeline, set up:

1. **Shader Stages**
2. **Fixed-Function States** (e.g., viewport, rasterizer, etc.)
3. **Pipeline Layout**

4. **Render Pass**

Create Pipeline Layout

```
VKPIPELINELAYOUTCREATEINFO pipelineLayoutInfo = {};

pipelineLayoutInfo.sType =
VK_STRUCTURE_TYPE_PIPELINE_LAYOUT_CREATE_INFO;

VkPipelineLayout pipelineLayout;

if (vkCreatePipelineLayout(device, &pipelineLayoutInfo, nullptr,
&pipelineLayout) != VK_SUCCESS) {

throw std::runtime_error("Failed to create pipeline layout!");

}
```

Configure the Pipeline

```
VKGRAPHICSPIPELINECREATEINFO pipelineInfo = {};

pipelineInfo.sType =
VK_STRUCTURE_TYPE_GRAPHICS_PIPELINE_CREATE_INFO

pipelineInfo.stageCount = 2;

pipelineInfo.pStages = shaderStages;

pipelineInfo.pVertexInputState = &vertexInputInfo;

pipelineInfo.pInputAssemblyState = &inputAssembly;

pipelineInfo.pViewportState = &viewportState;

pipelineInfo.pRasterizationState = &rasterizer;
```

```
pipelineInfo.pMultisampleState = &multisampling;

pipelineInfo.pColorBlendState = &colorBlending;

pipelineInfo.layout = pipelineLayout;

pipelineInfo.renderPass = renderPass;

pipelineInfo.subpass = 0;

if (vkCreateGraphicsPipelines(device, VK_NULL_HANDLE, 1, &pipelineInfo, nullptr, &graphicsPipeline) != VK_SUCCESS) {

throw std::runtime_error("Failed to create graphics pipeline!");

}
```

Step 5: Recording Command Buffers

RECORD COMMANDS TO draw the triangle into a command buffer.

```
VkCommandBufferBeginInfo beginInfo = {};

beginInfo.sType = VK_STRUCTURE_TYPE_COMMAND_BUFFER_BEGIN_INFO;

vkBeginCommandBuffer(commandBuffer, &beginInfo);

VkRenderPassBeginInfo renderPassInfo = {};

renderPassInfo.sType = VK_STRUCTURE_TYPE_RENDER_PASS_BEGIN_INFO;

renderPassInfo.renderPass = renderPass;

renderPassInfo.framebuffer = swapChainFramebuffers[i];
```

```
renderPassInfo.renderArea.offset = {0, 0};

renderPassInfo.renderArea.extent = swapChainExtent;

VkClearValue clearColor = {{{0.0f, 0.0f, 0.0f, 1.0f}}};

renderPassInfo.clearValueCount = 1;

renderPassInfo.pClearValues = &clearColor;

vkCmdBeginRenderPass(commandBuffer, &renderPassInfo, VK_SUBPASS_CONTENTS_INLINE);

vkCmdBindPipeline(commandBuffer, VK_PIPELINE_BIND_POINT_GRAPHICS, graphicsPipeline);

VkBuffer vertexBuffers[] = {vertexBuffer};

VkDeviceSize offsets[] = {0};

vkCmdBindVertexBuffers(commandBuffer, 0, 1, vertexBuffers, offsets);

vkCmdDraw(commandBuffer, 3, 1, 0, 0);

vkCmdEndRenderPass(commandBuffer);

vkEndCommandBuffer(commandBuffer);
```

Step 6: Drawing and Presenting

SUBMIT THE COMMAND buffer and present the rendered image to the swapchain.

Step 7: Synchronizing Rendering Operations

USE SEMAPHORES AND fences to synchronize between rendering and presentation.

This covers the complete process of rendering a triangle using Vulkan, introducing fundamental concepts necessary for more complex applications.

Synchronization Primitives

IN VULKAN, SYNCHRONIZATION is crucial to ensure the correct sequencing of operations across the GPU and CPU. Vulkan's lower-level control means you must explicitly manage synchronization to avoid issues like race conditions, data corruption, or undefined behavior. Unlike higher-level APIs where synchronization is hidden, Vulkan provides various primitives to achieve fine-grained control over execution flow.

This section covers key synchronization primitives in Vulkan:

1. **Semaphores**
2. **Fences**
3. **Events**
4. **Pipeline Barriers**

We'll explore each of these in detail, discussing their purpose, how to create and use them, and typical use cases.

Semaphores

SEMAPHORES ARE USED to synchronize the **order of operations** between different GPU queues. They ensure that one queue operation completes before another queue operation starts. Semaphores are most commonly used for synchronizing **image acquisition** and **presentation** in swapchain operations.

Creating Semaphores

TO CREATE A SEMAPHORE, use the VkSemaphoreCreateInfo structure:

```
VkSemaphore imageAvailableSemaphore;

VkSemaphore renderFinishedSemaphore;

VkSemaphoreCreateInfo semaphoreInfo = {};

semaphoreInfo.sType = VK_STRUCTURE_TYPE_SEMAPHORE_CREATE_INFO;

if (vkCreateSemaphore(device, &semaphoreInfo, nullptr, &imageAvailableSemaphore) != VK_SUCCESS ||

vkCreateSemaphore(device, &semaphoreInfo, nullptr, &renderFinishedSemaphore) != VK_SUCCESS) {

throw std::runtime_error("Failed to create semaphores!");

}
```

Here, we create two semaphores:

- imageAvailableSemaphore: Signals when an image from the swapchain is available for rendering.
- renderFinishedSemaphore: Signals when the rendering is complete and the image is ready to be presented.

Using Semaphores in Queue Submission

SEMAPHORES ARE SPECIFIED during command buffer submission to the graphics queue. Here's an example:

```
VkSubmitInfo submitInfo = {};

submitInfo.sType = VK_STRUCTURE_TYPE_SUBMIT_INFO;

VkSemaphore waitSemaphores[] = {imageAvailableSemaphore};

VkPipelineStageFlags waitStages[] = {VK_PIPELINE_STAGE_COLOR_ATTACHMENT_OUTPUT_BI

submitInfo.waitSemaphoreCount = 1;

submitInfo.pWaitSemaphores = waitSemaphores;

submitInfo.pWaitDstStageMask = waitStages;

submitInfo.commandBufferCount = 1;

submitInfo.pCommandBuffers = &commandBuffer;

VkSemaphore signalSemaphores[] = {renderFinishedSemaphore};

submitInfo.signalSemaphoreCount = 1;

submitInfo.pSignalSemaphores = signalSemaphores;

if (vkQueueSubmit(graphicsQueue, 1, &submitInfo, VK_NULL_HANDLE) != VK_SUCCESS) {

throw std::runtime_error("Failed to submit draw command buffer!");

}
```

In this example:

1. The queue waits on imageAvailableSemaphore to ensure the image is ready for rendering.

2. The renderFinishedSemaphore signals that rendering has finished.

Synchronizing Swapchain Presentation

AFTER SUBMITTING THE command buffer, the renderFinishedSemaphore is passed to vkQueuePresentKHR to ensure the image is presented only after rendering completes.

```
VkPresentInfoKHR presentInfo = {};

presentInfo.sType = VK_STRUCTURE_TYPE_PRESENT_INFO_KHR;

presentInfo.waitSemaphoreCount = 1;

presentInfo.pWaitSemaphores = &renderFinishedSemaphore;

VkSwapchainKHR swapChains[] = {swapchain};

presentInfo.swapchainCount = 1;

presentInfo.pSwapchains = swapChains;

presentInfo.pImageIndices = &imageIndex;

vkQueuePresentKHR(presentQueue, &presentInfo);
```

Fences

FENCES ARE USED TO synchronize between the **CPU and GPU**. They allow the CPU to wait until the GPU has finished executing a command buffer. Unlike semaphores, fences can be queried or waited upon by the CPU.

Creating Fences

```
VKFENCE RENDERFENCE;

VkFenceCreateInfo fenceInfo = {};

fenceInfo.sType =
VK_STRUCTURE_TYPE_FENCE_CREATE_INFO;

fenceInfo.flags = VK_FENCE_CREATE_SIGNALED_BIT;

if (vkCreateFence(device, &fenceInfo, nullptr, &renderFence) !=
VK_SUCCESS) {

throw std::runtime_error("Failed to create fence!");

}
```

The VK_FENCE_CREATE_SIGNALED_BIT flag initializes the fence in a signaled state, allowing for immediate reuse without waiting on the first frame.

Waiting on Fences

BEFORE REUSING A COMMAND buffer, wait for the fence to ensure the previous submission has finished:

```
vkWaitForFences(device, 1, &renderFence, VK_TRUE,
UINT64_MAX);

vkResetFences(device, 1, &renderFence);
```

This call blocks the CPU until the fence is signaled, meaning the GPU has finished the work associated with the fence.

Using Fences in Queue Submission

INCLUDE THE FENCE IN vkQueueSubmit to signal it when the GPU completes execution:

```
if (vkQueueSubmit(graphicsQueue, 1, &submitInfo, renderFence) != VK_SUCCESS) {
throw std::runtime_error("Failed to submit draw command buffer!");
}
```

Events

EVENTS ARE LIGHTWEIGHT synchronization primitives that can be set and reset by both the CPU and the GPU. They offer more flexibility than semaphores for fine-grained control within a single command buffer.

Creating Events

```
VKEVENT EVENT;

VkEventCreateInfo eventInfo = {};

eventInfo.sType = VK_STRUCTURE_TYPE_EVENT_CREATE_INFO;

if (vkCreateEvent(device, &eventInfo, nullptr, &event) != VK_SUCCESS) {

throw std::runtime_error("Failed to create event!");

}
```

Setting and Resetting Events

EVENTS CAN BE SET AND reset by the CPU using:

vkSetEvent(device, event);

vkResetEvent(device, event);

Using Events in Command Buffers

WITHIN A COMMAND BUFFER, you can use vkCmdSetEvent and vkCmdWaitEvents:

vkCmdSetEvent(commandBuffer, event, VK_PIPELINE_STAGE_COLOR_ATTACHMENT_OUTPUT_BI

vkCmdWaitEvents(

commandBuffer, 1, &event,

VK_PIPELINE_STAGE_COLOR_ATTACHMENT_OUTPUT_BI

VK_PIPELINE_STAGE_FRAGMENT_SHADER_BIT,

0, nullptr, 0, nullptr, 0, nullptr

);

This ensures that subsequent operations in the fragment shader stage wait for the color attachment output stage to complete.

Pipeline Barriers

PIPELINE BARRIERS SYNCHRONIZE access to resources (buffers or images) and ensure correct ordering of operations within a single command buffer. They help transition resources between different states.

Example of a Pipeline Barrier

```
VKIMAGEMEMORYBARRIER barrier = {};

barrier.sType = VK_STRUCTURE_TYPE_IMAGE_MEMORY_BARRIER;

barrier.oldLayout = VK_IMAGE_LAYOUT_UNDEFINED;

barrier.newLayout = VK_IMAGE_LAYOUT_COLOR_ATTACHMENT_OPTIMAL;

barrier.srcQueueFamilyIndex = VK_QUEUE_FAMILY_IGNORED;

barrier.dstQueueFamilyIndex = VK_QUEUE_FAMILY_IGNORED;

barrier.image = image;

barrier.subresourceRange.aspectMask = VK_IMAGE_ASPECT_COLOR_BIT;

barrier.subresourceRange.baseMipLevel = 0;

barrier.subresourceRange.levelCount = 1;

barrier.subresourceRange.baseArrayLayer = 0;

barrier.subresourceRange.layerCount = 1;

barrier.srcAccessMask = 0;
```

barrier.dstAccessMask =
VK_ACCESS_COLOR_ATTACHMENT_WRITE_BIT;

vkCmdPipelineBarrier(

commandBuffer,

VK_PIPELINE_STAGE_TOP_OF_PIPE_BIT, // Source stage

VK_PIPELINE_STAGE_COLOR_ATTACHMENT_OUTPUT_BIT
// Destination stage

0,

0, nullptr,

0, nullptr,

1, &barrier

);

In this example:

1. The image layout is transitioned from VK_IMAGE_LAYOUT_UNDEFINED to VK_IMAGE_LAYOUT_COLOR_ATTACHMENT_OPTI
2. The pipeline stages are specified to ensure the transition happens before the color attachment output stage.

Conclusion

SYNCHRONIZATION PRIMITIVES in Vulkan provide powerful control over execution flow. Understanding how to use semaphores, fences, events, and pipeline barriers is crucial for managing complex rendering operations and avoiding race conditions. By mastering these tools, you can ensure your Vulkan applications run efficiently and reliably.

Chapter 6: Advanced Vulkan Rendering Techniques

Depth and Stencil Buffers

DEPTH AND STENCIL BUFFERS are essential tools in Vulkan for managing rendering accuracy and enabling advanced visual effects. They help ensure proper occlusion and allow for intricate masking operations during rendering. This section covers the fundamentals, setup, and common use cases of depth and stencil buffers.

Depth Buffer Fundamentals

THE DEPTH BUFFER, ALSO known as a *z-buffer*, is a dedicated buffer that stores depth information for each pixel. Its primary function is to determine the visibility of pixels based on their distance from the camera.

When a pixel is drawn, Vulkan compares the new pixel's depth value with the existing value in the depth buffer:

- **If the new depth is closer** (i.e., the pixel is in front of the existing one), the new pixel is drawn, and the depth buffer is updated.

- **If the new depth is farther**, the pixel is discarded, and the depth buffer remains unchanged.

Depth Buffer Precision

DEPTH BUFFER PRECISION is typically determined by the bit-depth of the buffer. Common formats include:

- **16-bit depth**: Offers lower precision but consumes less memory.
- **24-bit depth**: A balanced option that provides good precision for most applications.
- **32-bit depth**: Offers the highest precision but requires more memory and may impact performance.

Depth Testing in Vulkan

DEPTH TESTING IS MANAGED through the VkPipelineDepthStencilStateCreateInfo structure. To enable depth testing in Vulkan, you typically configure the following fields:

- **depthTestEnable**: Whether depth testing is enabled (VK_TRUE or VK_FALSE).
- **depthWriteEnable**: Whether depth writes are enabled.
- **depthCompareOp**: The comparison function to use (e.g., VK_COMPARE_OP_LESS).
- **depthBoundsTestEnable**: Whether to perform depth bounds testing.
- **stencilTestEnable**: Whether to enable stencil testing.

Here's an example of how to configure depth testing in Vulkan:

VkPipelineDepthStencilStateCreateInfo depthStencil = {};

depthStencil.sType = VK_STRUCTURE_TYPE_PIPELINE_DEPTH_STENCIL_STATE_C

```
depthStencil.depthTestEnable = VK_TRUE;
depthStencil.depthWriteEnable = VK_TRUE;
depthStencil.depthCompareOp = VK_COMPARE_OP_LESS;
depthStencil.depthBoundsTestEnable = VK_FALSE;
depthStencil.stencilTestEnable = VK_FALSE;
depthStencil.minDepthBounds = 0.0f;
depthStencil.maxDepthBounds = 1.0f;
```

In this configuration:

- Depth testing is enabled.
- Depth writes are enabled to update the depth buffer.
- The comparison function is set to VK_COMPARE_OP_LESS, meaning the new depth must be less than the stored depth to pass the test.

Creating a Depth Buffer

CREATING A DEPTH BUFFER in Vulkan involves several steps:

1. **Create a depth image**: The depth buffer is implemented as an image with a suitable depth format.
2. **Allocate memory**: Allocate and bind memory for the depth image.
3. **Create an image view**: Create an image view for the depth image to use it in the pipeline.
4. **Transition the image layout**: Transition the depth image

to
VK_IMAGE_LAYOUT_DEPTH_STENCIL_ATTACHMEN

Choosing a Depth Format

COMMON DEPTH FORMATS in Vulkan include:

- **VK_FORMAT_D16_UNORM**: 16-bit depth format.
- **VK_FORMAT_D24_UNORM_S8_UINT**: 24-bit depth with an 8-bit stencil component.
- **VK_FORMAT_D32_SFLOAT**: 32-bit depth with floating-point precision.

To find a suitable depth format, you can use the following function:

```
VkFormat findDepthFormat(VkPhysicalDevice physicalDevice) {

VkFormat candidates[] = {VK_FORMAT_D32_SFLOAT,
VK_FORMAT_D24_UNORM_S8_UINT,
VK_FORMAT_D16_UNORM};

for (VkFormat format : candidates) {

VkFormatProperties props;

vkGetPhysicalDeviceFormatProperties(physicalDevice, format,
&props);

if (props.optimalTilingFeatures &
VK_FORMAT_FEATURE_DEPTH_STENCIL_ATTACHMENT_BI
{

return format;
```

```
}
}
throw std::runtime_error("Failed to find a supported depth format!");
}
```

Creating the Depth Image

HERE'S AN EXAMPLE OF creating a depth image:

```
VkImageCreateInfo imageInfo = {};
imageInfo.sType = VK_STRUCTURE_TYPE_IMAGE_CREATE_INFO;
imageInfo.imageType = VK_IMAGE_TYPE_2D;
imageInfo.extent.width = swapChainExtent.width;
imageInfo.extent.height = swapChainExtent.height;
imageInfo.extent.depth = 1;
imageInfo.mipLevels = 1;
imageInfo.arrayLayers = 1;
imageInfo.format = depthFormat;
imageInfo.tiling = VK_IMAGE_TILING_OPTIMAL;
imageInfo.initialLayout = VK_IMAGE_LAYOUT_UNDEFINED;
```

imageInfo.usage = VK_IMAGE_USAGE_DEPTH_STENCIL_ATTACHMENT_BIT;

imageInfo.samples = VK_SAMPLE_COUNT_1_BIT;

imageInfo.sharingMode = VK_SHARING_MODE_EXCLUSIVE;

if (vkCreateImage(device, &imageInfo, nullptr, &depthImage) != VK_SUCCESS) {

throw std::runtime_error("Failed to create depth image!");

}

Allocating Memory for the Depth Image

AFTER CREATING THE image, allocate memory for it:

VkMemoryRequirements memRequirements;

vkGetImageMemoryRequirements(device, depthImage, &memRequirements);

VkMemoryAllocateInfo allocInfo = {};

allocInfo.sType = VK_STRUCTURE_TYPE_MEMORY_ALLOCATE_INFO;

allocInfo.allocationSize = memRequirements.size;

allocInfo.memoryTypeIndex = findMemoryType(memRequirements.memoryTypeBits, VK_MEMORY_PROPERTY_DEVICE_LOCAL_BIT);

if (vkAllocateMemory(device, &allocInfo, nullptr, &depthImageMemory) != VK_SUCCESS) {

throw std::runtime_error("Failed to allocate depth image memory!");

}

vkBindImageMemory(device, depthImage, depthImageMemory, 0);

Creating the Depth Image View

CREATE AN IMAGE VIEW for the depth image:

VkImageViewCreateInfo viewInfo = {};

viewInfo.sType = VK_STRUCTURE_TYPE_IMAGE_VIEW_CREATE_INFO;

viewInfo.image = depthImage;

viewInfo.viewType = VK_IMAGE_VIEW_TYPE_2D;

viewInfo.format = depthFormat;

viewInfo.subresourceRange.aspectMask = VK_IMAGE_ASPECT_DEPTH_BIT;

viewInfo.subresourceRange.baseMipLevel = 0;

viewInfo.subresourceRange.levelCount = 1;

viewInfo.subresourceRange.baseArrayLayer = 0;

viewInfo.subresourceRange.layerCount = 1;

if (vkCreateImageView(device, &viewInfo, nullptr, &depthImageView) != VK_SUCCESS) {

throw std::runtime_error("Failed to create depth image view!");

}

Depth Biasing

DEPTH BIASING IS USEFUL for techniques like shadow mapping, where small precision errors can cause surface acne (self-shadowing artifacts).

To apply depth biasing in Vulkan:

1. **Set depthBiasEnable to VK_TRUE.**
2. **Configure depthBiasConstantFactor** (constant bias) and depthBiasSlopeFactor** (slope bias).

Example configuration:

rasterizer.depthBiasEnable = VK_TRUE;

rasterizer.depthBiasConstantFactor = 1.25f;

rasterizer.depthBiasSlopeFactor = 1.75f;

Stencil Buffer Fundamentals

THE STENCIL BUFFER allows for masking operations during rendering. It operates similarly to the depth buffer but stores integer values for each pixel.

Common use cases include:

- **Shadow volumes.**
- **Outlining objects.**
- **Complex masking effects.**

Stencil operations are defined in VkStencilOpState structures, which specify how the stencil test behaves.

Multi-Sampling Anti-Aliasing (MSAA)

MULTI-SAMPLING ANTI-Aliasing (MSAA) is a technique used to reduce jagged edges, or "aliasing," in computer graphics. Aliasing occurs when high-frequency detail, such as the edge of a polygon, is undersampled, causing a jagged appearance. MSAA smooths these edges by sampling multiple points within each pixel and blending the results. This approach strikes a balance between image quality and performance compared to more expensive full-screen anti-aliasing techniques.

In this section, we'll cover the theory behind MSAA, how to enable it in Vulkan, and practical implementation steps. Additionally, we'll explore trade-offs and optimization strategies for MSAA in real-world applications.

How MSAA Works

IN TRADITIONAL RASTERIZATION, each pixel on the screen corresponds to a single sample point, typically located at the center of the pixel. This means that a polygon either fully covers the sample point or does not cover it at all, leading to hard, jagged edges.

MSAA improves upon this by increasing the number of sample points within each pixel. For example:

- **2x MSAA**: Two sample points per pixel.
- **4x MSAA**: Four sample points per pixel.
- **8x MSAA**: Eight sample points per pixel.

The key idea of MSAA is that **fragment shaders are executed once per pixel**, but coverage is determined for each sample point. The results are then combined based on the proportion of samples that fall within the polygon.

For example, with 4x MSAA, if a polygon covers two of the four sample points in a pixel, the final color of the pixel is blended with 50% of the polygon's color and 50% of the background color.

Configuring MSAA in Vulkan

ENABLING MSAA IN VULKAN requires several steps, including selecting a sample count, creating appropriate image resources, and configuring the pipeline to use multi-sampling.

Step 1: Selecting a Sample Count

VULKAN SUPPORTS DIFFERENT sample counts depending on the capabilities of the GPU. Common options are:

- VK_SAMPLE_COUNT_1_BIT: No MSAA (single sample).
- VK_SAMPLE_COUNT_2_BIT: 2x MSAA.
- VK_SAMPLE_COUNT_4_BIT: 4x MSAA.
- VK_SAMPLE_COUNT_8_BIT: 8x MSAA.

To determine the highest supported sample count, query the physical device's properties:

VkPhysicalDeviceProperties physicalDeviceProperties;

```
vkGetPhysicalDeviceProperties(physicalDevice,
&physicalDeviceProperties);

VkSampleCountFlags getMaxUsableSampleCount() {

VkSampleCountFlags counts =
physicalDeviceProperties.limits.framebufferColorSampleCounts &
physicalDeviceProperties.limits.framebufferDepthSampleCounts;

if (counts & VK_SAMPLE_COUNT_64_BIT) { return
VK_SAMPLE_COUNT_64_BIT; }

if (counts & VK_SAMPLE_COUNT_32_BIT) { return
VK_SAMPLE_COUNT_32_BIT; }

if (counts & VK_SAMPLE_COUNT_16_BIT) { return
VK_SAMPLE_COUNT_16_BIT; }

if (counts & VK_SAMPLE_COUNT_8_BIT) { return
VK_SAMPLE_COUNT_8_BIT; }

if (counts & VK_SAMPLE_COUNT_4_BIT) { return
VK_SAMPLE_COUNT_4_BIT; }

if (counts & VK_SAMPLE_COUNT_2_BIT) { return
VK_SAMPLE_COUNT_2_BIT; }

return VK_SAMPLE_COUNT_1_BIT;

}

VkSampleCountFlagBits msaaSamples =
getMaxUsableSampleCount();
```

This function checks the maximum sample count supported by the GPU for both color and depth attachments and selects the highest available option.

Step 2: Creating MSAA-Compatible Image Resources

TO USE MSAA, YOU NEED to create additional image resources for the color buffer and depth buffer that support multi-sampling.

Creating a Multi-Sampled Color Image

HERE'S AN EXAMPLE OF creating a multi-sampled color image:

```
VkImageCreateInfo colorImageInfo = {};

colorImageInfo.sType = VK_STRUCTURE_TYPE_IMAGE_CREATE_INFO;

colorImageInfo.imageType = VK_IMAGE_TYPE_2D;

colorImageInfo.extent.width = swapChainExtent.width;

colorImageInfo.extent.height = swapChainExtent.height;

colorImageInfo.extent.depth = 1;

colorImageInfo.mipLevels = 1;

colorImageInfo.arrayLayers = 1;

colorImageInfo.format = swapChainImageFormat;

colorImageInfo.samples = msaaSamples; // Use the selected MSAA sample count

colorImageInfo.tiling = VK_IMAGE_TILING_OPTIMAL;

colorImageInfo.usage = VK_IMAGE_USAGE_TRANSIENT_ATTACHMENT_BIT | VK_IMAGE_USAGE_COLOR_ATTACHMENT_BIT;
```

```
colorImageInfo.sharingMode = VK_SHARING_MODE_EXCLUSIVE;

colorImageInfo.initialLayout = VK_IMAGE_LAYOUT_UNDEFINED;

if (vkCreateImage(device, &colorImageInfo, nullptr, &colorImage) != VK_SUCCESS) {

throw std::runtime_error("Failed to create multi-sampled color image!");

}
```

Allocating Memory for the Multi-Sampled Image

ALLOCATE MEMORY FOR the multi-sampled color image similarly to a standard image:

```
VkMemoryRequirements memRequirements;

vkGetImageMemoryRequirements(device, colorImage, &memRequirements);

VkMemoryAllocateInfo allocInfo = {};

allocInfo.sType = VK_STRUCTURE_TYPE_MEMORY_ALLOCATE_INFO;

allocInfo.allocationSize = memRequirements.size;

allocInfo.memoryTypeIndex = findMemoryType(memRequirements.memoryTypeBits, VK_MEMORY_PROPERTY_DEVICE_LOCAL_BIT);
```

if (vkAllocateMemory(device, &allocInfo, nullptr, &colorImageMemory) != VK_SUCCESS) {

throw std::runtime_error("Failed to allocate memory for multi-sampled color image!");

}

vkBindImageMemory(device, colorImage, colorImageMemory, 0);

Creating a Multi-Sampled Image View

CREATE AN IMAGE VIEW for the multi-sampled color image:

VkImageViewCreateInfo colorImageViewInfo = {};

colorImageViewInfo.sType = VK_STRUCTURE_TYPE_IMAGE_VIEW_CREATE_INFO;

colorImageViewInfo.image = colorImage;

colorImageViewInfo.viewType = VK_IMAGE_VIEW_TYPE_2D;

colorImageViewInfo.format = swapChainImageFormat;

colorImageViewInfo.subresourceRange.aspectMask = VK_IMAGE_ASPECT_COLOR_BIT;

colorImageViewInfo.subresourceRange.baseMipLevel = 0;

colorImageViewInfo.subresourceRange.levelCount = 1;

colorImageViewInfo.subresourceRange.baseArrayLayer = 0;

colorImageViewInfo.subresourceRange.layerCount = 1;

if (vkCreateImageView(device, &colorImageViewInfo, nullptr, &colorImageView) != VK_SUCCESS) {

throw std::runtime_error("Failed to create multi-sampled color image view!");

}

Step 3: Configuring the Pipeline for MSAA

TO ENABLE MSAA IN THE graphics pipeline, configure the VkPipelineMultisampleStateCreateInfo structure:

VkPipelineMultisampleStateCreateInfo multisampling = {};

multisampling.sType = VK_STRUCTURE_TYPE_PIPELINE_MULTISAMPLE_STATE_C

multisampling.sampleShadingEnable = VK_FALSE;

multisampling.rasterizationSamples = msaaSamples;

multisampling.minSampleShading = 1.0f;

multisampling.pSampleMask = nullptr;

multisampling.alphaToCoverageEnable = VK_FALSE;

multisampling.alphaToOneEnable = VK_FALSE;

Add this configuration to your pipeline creation process.

Step 4: Resolving the Multi-Sampled Image

SINCE THE SWAPCHAIN images do not support multi-sampling, you need to resolve the multi-sampled image into a single-sampled image before presenting it. This can be done using a resolve attachment in the render pass.

In the VkSubpassDescription, set up both the color attachment (multi-sampled) and the resolve attachment (single-sampled):

```
VkAttachmentReference colorAttachmentRef = {0, VK_IMAGE_LAYOUT_COLOR_ATTACHMENT_OPTIMAL};

VkAttachmentReference resolveAttachmentRef = {1, VK_IMAGE_LAYOUT_COLOR_ATTACHMENT_OPTIMAL};

VkSubpassDescription subpass = {};

subpass.pipelineBindPoint = VK_PIPELINE_BIND_POINT_GRAPHICS;

subpass.colorAttachmentCount = 1;

subpass.pColorAttachments = &colorAttachmentRef;

subpass.pResolveAttachments = &resolveAttachmentRef;
```

Trade-Offs and Performance Considerations

WHILE MSAA PROVIDES significant improvements in image quality, it comes with performance costs. The higher the sample count, the greater the memory usage and processing time. Some considerations include:

- **2x MSAA** offers modest quality improvements with minimal performance impact.
- **4x MSAA** is a common choice for balancing quality and performance.
- **8x MSAA** provides excellent quality but may not be suitable for performance-critical applications.

For mobile or low-power devices, lower sample counts or alternative techniques like FXAA (Fast Approximate Anti-Aliasing) might be preferable.

Conclusion

MULTI-SAMPLING ANTI-Aliasing (MSAA) is an effective method for reducing aliasing in Vulkan applications. By understanding how to select sample counts, configure images, and set up the pipeline, you can achieve smoother visuals while balancing performance.

Post-Processing Effects

POST-PROCESSING EFFECTS are techniques applied to rendered images after the initial rendering stage to enhance visual quality, create special effects, or improve realism. These effects are commonly used in games, simulations, and visualization applications to achieve cinematic visuals or stylistic transformations. In Vulkan, post-processing effects are typically implemented through fragment shaders or compute shaders that operate on rendered textures.

In this section, we will explore common post-processing techniques, their implementation in Vulkan, and key considerations for optimizing these effects. We'll cover effects such as bloom, screen-space ambient occlusion (SSAO), color correction, depth of field, and motion blur.

Setting Up Post-Processing in Vulkan

TO APPLY POST-PROCESSING effects, the rendering workflow generally includes these steps:

1. **Render the scene to an offscreen framebuffer** (instead of

directly to the swapchain).
2. **Bind the resulting color attachment as a texture** for post-processing.
3. **Apply post-processing shaders** using a full-screen quad.
4. **Render the final processed image** to the swapchain for display.

Creating an Offscreen Framebuffer

FIRST, CREATE AN OFFSCREEN framebuffer with attachments for color and depth. Here's an example of setting up an offscreen framebuffer:

```
VkImageCreateInfo offscreenImageInfo = {};

offscreenImageInfo.sType = VK_STRUCTURE_TYPE_IMAGE_CREATE_INFO;

offscreenImageInfo.imageType = VK_IMAGE_TYPE_2D;

offscreenImageInfo.extent.width = swapChainExtent.width;

offscreenImageInfo.extent.height = swapChainExtent.height;

offscreenImageInfo.extent.depth = 1;

offscreenImageInfo.mipLevels = 1;

offscreenImageInfo.arrayLayers = 1;

offscreenImageInfo.format = VK_FORMAT_R8G8B8A8_UNORM;

offscreenImageInfo.samples = VK_SAMPLE_COUNT_1_BIT;

offscreenImageInfo.tiling = VK_IMAGE_TILING_OPTIMAL;
```

```
offscreenImageInfo.usage = VK_IMAGE_USAGE_COLOR_ATTACHMENT_BIT | VK_IMAGE_USAGE_SAMPLED_BIT;

offscreenImageInfo.initialLayout = VK_IMAGE_LAYOUT_UNDEFINED;

vkCreateImage(device, &offscreenImageInfo, nullptr, &offscreenImage);
```

Allocate memory and create an image view for the offscreen image. Then, create a framebuffer that uses this image as a color attachment.

Rendering a Full-Screen Quad

TO APPLY POST-PROCESSING, you need to render a full-screen quad that covers the entire viewport. This quad is drawn in screen space and is textured with the offscreen image.

Define the vertices for the full-screen quad:

```
std::vector<Vertex> quadVertices = {

{{-1.0f, -1.0f, 0.0f}, {0.0f, 0.0f}}, // Bottom-left

{{1.0f, -1.0f, 0.0f}, {1.0f, 0.0f}}, // Bottom-right

{{-1.0f, 1.0f, 0.0f}, {0.0f, 1.0f}}, // Top-left

{{1.0f, 1.0f, 0.0f}, {1.0f, 1.0f}} // Top-right

};
```

Set up the vertex and fragment shaders to render this quad. The fragment shader will apply the post-processing effect.

Bloom Effect

BLOOM IS A POST-PROCESSING effect that creates a glowing effect around bright areas of the image. It simulates light scattering, making bright objects appear to emit light.

Steps to Implement Bloom

1. **Extract Bright Areas**: Render only the bright parts of the scene to a separate texture.
2. **Blur the Bright Texture**: Apply a Gaussian blur to the bright texture.
3. **Combine with Original Image**: Blend the blurred texture with the original image.

Brightness Extraction Shader

THE BRIGHTNESS EXTRACTION shader isolates pixels that are above a certain brightness threshold:

```
#version 450

layout(binding = 0) uniform sampler2D inputImage;

layout(location = 0) in vec2 fragUV;

layout(location = 0) out vec4 outColor;

void main() {

vec3 color = texture(inputImage, fragUV).rgb;

float brightness = dot(color, vec3(0.299, 0.587, 0.114));

if (brightness > 1.0) {
```

```
outColor = vec4(color, 1.0);

} else {

outColor = vec4(0.0);

}

}
```

Gaussian Blur Shader

THE BLUR SHADER APPLIES a Gaussian blur in horizontal and vertical passes:

```
#version 450

layout(binding = 0) uniform sampler2D image;

layout(location = 0) in vec2 fragUV;

layout(location = 0) out vec4 outColor;

const float weights[5] = float[](0.227, 0.194, 0.121, 0.054, 0.016);

const float offsets[5] = float[](0.0, 1.0, 2.0, 3.0, 4.0);

void main() {

vec3 result = texture(image, fragUV).rgb * weights[0];

for (int i = 1; i < 5; i++) {

result += texture(image, fragUV + vec2(offsets[i], 0.0) / textureSize(image, 0)).rgb * weights[i];

result += texture(image, fragUV - vec2(offsets[i], 0.0) / textureSize(image, 0)).rgb * weights[i];
```

```
}
outColor = vec4(result, 1.0);
}
```

Combining Bloom with the Original Image

FINALLY, BLEND THE blurred image with the original scene:

```
#version 450
layout(binding = 0) uniform sampler2D originalImage;
layout(binding = 1) uniform sampler2D bloomImage;
layout(location = 0) in vec2 fragUV;
layout(location = 0) out vec4 outColor;
void main() {
vec3 original = texture(originalImage, fragUV).rgb;
vec3 bloom = texture(bloomImage, fragUV).rgb;
outColor = vec4(original + bloom, 1.0);
}
```

Screen-Space Ambient Occlusion (SSAO)

SSAO IS A POST-PROCESSING technique that approximates how ambient light is occluded by nearby surfaces, adding realistic shadowing to crevices and corners.

SSAO Steps

1. **Generate Random Samples**: Create a set of sample points in a hemisphere.
2. **Calculate Occlusion**: For each pixel, compare the depth of the surrounding samples to determine occlusion.
3. **Blur and Combine**: Blur the occlusion map and combine it with the scene.

Color Correction

COLOR CORRECTION ADJUSTS the colors of the rendered image to achieve a specific look or mood. This can include operations like brightness, contrast, saturation, and applying color grading filters.

Color Correction Shader

```
#VERSION 450

layout(binding = 0) uniform sampler2D inputImage;

layout(location = 0) in vec2 fragUV;

layout(location = 0) out vec4 outColor;

uniform float brightness;

uniform float contrast;

uniform float saturation;

vec3 adjustSaturation(vec3 color, float saturation) {

float grey = dot(color, vec3(0.299, 0.587, 0.114));
```

```
return mix(vec3(grey), color, saturation);
}
void main() {
vec3 color = texture(inputImage, fragUV).rgb;
color = color * brightness;
color = (color - 0.5) * contrast + 0.5;
color = adjustSaturation(color, saturation);
outColor = vec4(color, 1.0);
}
```

Conclusion

POST-PROCESSING EFFECTS are powerful tools in Vulkan that can dramatically enhance the visual fidelity of your applications. By understanding and implementing effects like bloom, SSAO, depth of field, and color correction, you can achieve professional-quality graphics and customize the visual style of your projects. Optimizing these effects for performance is crucial, especially in real-time applications, to maintain a balance between quality and efficiency.

Chapter 7: Vulkan Compute Operations

Introduction to Compute Shaders

COMPUTE SHADERS IN Vulkan provide a way to perform general-purpose computation on the GPU. Unlike traditional vertex and fragment shaders, compute shaders are not restricted to graphics rendering. They allow you to leverage the massive parallelism of modern GPUs for tasks like physics simulations, image processing, particle systems, and artificial intelligence. Compute shaders are part of the programmable pipeline, enabling developers to write highly parallel code for data processing.

This section explores the fundamentals of compute shaders, how to create and execute them in Vulkan, and practical examples of using compute shaders for real-world applications.

What Are Compute Shaders?

COMPUTE SHADERS ARE a type of shader program executed by the GPU for general-purpose computations. They operate on large datasets by dividing the work into smaller units called **workgroups**. Each workgroup contains multiple **invocations**, which are individual threads that execute the shader code in parallel.

Key concepts of compute shaders include:

1. **Workgroups**: Groups of threads (invocations) that operate together on a shared set of data.
2. **Local Invocation IDs**: Identifiers for threads within a workgroup.
3. **Global Invocation IDs**: Unique identifiers for threads

across all workgroups.

4. **Shared Memory**: Fast memory accessible by all threads within a workgroup.

Compute Shader Execution Model

WHEN A COMPUTE SHADER is dispatched, Vulkan divides the work into a grid of workgroups. Each workgroup is processed independently, and within each workgroup, threads execute concurrently. The work is dispatched using a **dispatch command** specifying the number of workgroups in each dimension.

Creating a Compute Shader in Vulkan

TO USE A COMPUTE SHADER in Vulkan, follow these steps:

1. **Write the compute shader code** in GLSL (GL Shading Language).
2. **Compile the shader** to SPIR-V format.
3. **Create a shader module** in Vulkan.
4. **Set up a compute pipeline.**
5. **Dispatch the compute shader.**

Let's go through these steps in detail.

Step 1: Writing the Compute Shader

HERE'S A BASIC EXAMPLE of a compute shader that adds two vectors:

```
#version 450

layout(local_size_x = 256) in; // 256 threads per workgroup
```

```
layout(set = 0, binding = 0) buffer InputA {
float a[];
};
layout(set = 0, binding = 1) buffer InputB {
float b[];
};
layout(set = 0, binding = 2) buffer Output {
float result[];
};
void main() {
uint idx = gl_GlobalInvocationID.x;
result[idx] = a[idx] + b[idx];
}
```

In this shader:

- **local_size_x = 256** defines that each workgroup contains 256 threads.
- The shader reads from two input buffers (a and b) and writes the sum to an output buffer (result).

Step 2: Compiling the Shader to SPIR-V

USE GLSLANGVALIDATOR to compile the GLSL compute shader to SPIR-V:

glslangValidator -V compute_shader.glsl -o compute_shader.spv

This generates a SPIR-V binary compute_shader.spv that Vulkan can use.

Step 3: Creating a Shader Module

CREATE A SHADER MODULE from the SPIR-V binary in your Vulkan application:

```
VkShaderModule createShaderModule(const std::vector<char>& code) {

VkShaderModuleCreateInfo createInfo = {};

createInfo.sType = VK_STRUCTURE_TYPE_SHADER_MODULE_CREATE_INFO;

createInfo.codeSize = code.size();

createInfo.pCode = reinterpret_cast<const uint32_t*>(code.data());

VkShaderModule shaderModule;

if (vkCreateShaderModule(device, &createInfo, nullptr, &shaderModule) != VK_SUCCESS) {

throw std::runtime_error("Failed to create shader module!");

}
```

```
return shaderModule;
}
```

Load the SPIR-V binary and create the shader module:

```
auto computeShaderCode = readFile("compute_shader.spv");
VkShaderModule computeShaderModule = createShaderModule(computeShaderCode);
```

Step 4: Setting Up the Compute Pipeline

CREATE A COMPUTE PIPELINE using the shader module:

```
VkPipelineShaderStageCreateInfo shaderStageInfo = {};
shaderStageInfo.sType = VK_STRUCTURE_TYPE_PIPELINE_SHADER_STAGE_CREATE
shaderStageInfo.stage = VK_SHADER_STAGE_COMPUTE_BIT;
shaderStageInfo.module = computeShaderModule;
shaderStageInfo.pName = "main";
VkComputePipelineCreateInfo pipelineInfo = {};
pipelineInfo.sType = VK_STRUCTURE_TYPE_COMPUTE_PIPELINE_CREATE_INF
pipelineInfo.stage = shaderStageInfo;
pipelineInfo.layout = pipelineLayout; // Create a pipeline layout with descriptor sets
```

```
VkPipeline computePipeline;

if (vkCreateComputePipelines(device, VK_NULL_HANDLE, 1,
&pipelineInfo, nullptr, &computePipeline) != VK_SUCCESS) {

throw std::runtime_error("Failed to create compute pipeline!");

}
```

Step 5: Dispatching the Compute Shader

RECORD A COMMAND TO dispatch the compute shader. Specify the number of workgroups:

```
vkCmdBindPipeline(commandBuffer,
VK_PIPELINE_BIND_POINT_COMPUTE,
computePipeline);

vkCmdBindDescriptorSets(commandBuffer,
VK_PIPELINE_BIND_POINT_COMPUTE, pipelineLayout, 0,
1, &descriptorSet, 0, nullptr);

// Dispatch with enough workgroups to cover the data size

uint32_t numElements = 1024;

vkCmdDispatch(commandBuffer, (numElements + 255) / 256, 1,
1);
```

In this example, if numElements is 1024, the dispatch call creates 4 workgroups ((1024 + 255) / 256).

Synchronization in Compute Shaders

COMPUTE OPERATIONS may need synchronization, especially when accessing buffers or images that are also used by graphics operations. Use pipeline barriers to ensure correct ordering.

Example barrier for a buffer:

VkBufferMemoryBarrier bufferBarrier = {};

bufferBarrier.sType = VK_STRUCTURE_TYPE_BUFFER_MEMORY_BARRIER;

bufferBarrier.srcAccessMask = VK_ACCESS_SHADER_WRITE_BIT;

bufferBarrier.dstAccessMask = VK_ACCESS_SHADER_READ_BIT;

bufferBarrier.srcQueueFamilyIndex = VK_QUEUE_FAMILY_IGNORED;

bufferBarrier.dstQueueFamilyIndex = VK_QUEUE_FAMILY_IGNORED;

bufferBarrier.buffer = outputBuffer;

bufferBarrier.offset = 0;

bufferBarrier.size = VK_WHOLE_SIZE;

vkCmdPipelineBarrier(

commandBuffer,

VK_PIPELINE_STAGE_COMPUTE_SHADER_BIT,

VK_PIPELINE_STAGE_VERTEX_SHADER_BIT,

```
0,
0, nullptr,
1, &bufferBarrier,
0, nullptr
);
```

Practical Use Cases for Compute Shaders

1. **Physics Simulations**: Compute shaders can simulate complex physical systems, such as fluid dynamics or particle systems.
2. **Image Processing**: Effects like Gaussian blur, edge detection, and HDR tonemapping can be efficiently implemented using compute shaders.
3. **AI and Machine Learning**: Compute shaders can accelerate inference tasks by performing parallel computations on large datasets.
4. **Post-Processing Effects**: Advanced effects like bloom, SSAO, and depth-of-field can be implemented using compute shaders for flexibility and performance.

Conclusion

COMPUTE SHADERS IN Vulkan offer powerful capabilities for general-purpose computation on the GPU. By understanding the principles of workgroups, synchronization, and efficient data management, you can leverage compute shaders to accelerate a wide range of tasks beyond traditional graphics rendering.

Offloading Workloads to Compute Pipelines

IN MODERN GRAPHICS and simulation applications, efficiently distributing workloads between different parts of the GPU is essential for maximizing performance. Vulkan's compute pipelines enable developers to offload a variety of tasks from the graphics pipeline to dedicated compute shaders. This offloading helps parallelize processing, reduce bottlenecks, and leverage the full potential of the GPU.

Compute pipelines are particularly useful for tasks such as physics simulations, AI computations, particle systems, and image processing. This section explores how to offload these workloads effectively to compute pipelines in Vulkan and optimize their execution.

Understanding the Compute Pipeline in Vulkan

THE COMPUTE PIPELINE in Vulkan is a separate execution path from the traditional graphics pipeline. While the graphics pipeline handles vertex, tessellation, and fragment shaders for rendering images, the compute pipeline executes compute shaders for general-purpose processing tasks.

Key concepts in the compute pipeline:

1. **Compute Shaders**: Programs that run on the GPU for non-graphics tasks.
2. **Workgroups**: Units of parallel execution in compute shaders.
3. **Pipeline Layout**: Describes the resources (e.g., buffers, images) available to the compute shader.
4. **Descriptor Sets**: Bind resources like buffers and images to the compute shader.

5. **Dispatch Commands**: Launch compute shader execution with specified workgroup dimensions.

The basic steps to use a compute pipeline are:

1. **Create a compute shader** and compile it to SPIR-V.
2. **Set up a compute pipeline** and bind the necessary resources.
3. **Dispatch the compute shader** with the appropriate workgroups.
4. **Synchronize** with other pipeline stages if necessary.

Creating a Compute Pipeline

Step 1: Writing a Compute Shader

LET'S WRITE A COMPUTE shader that performs a simple physics simulation by updating particle positions based on velocity and time:

```
#version 450

layout(local_size_x = 256) in; // 256 threads per workgroup

struct Particle {

vec2 position;

vec2 velocity;

};

layout(set = 0, binding = 0) buffer Particles {

Particle particles[];
```

```
};
uniform float deltaTime;
void main() {
uint idx = gl_GlobalInvocationID.x;
particles[idx].position += particles[idx].velocity * deltaTime;
}
```

In this shader:

- **local_size_x = 256**: Each workgroup has 256 threads.
- **Particle**: A struct containing position and velocity vectors.
- **deltaTime**: A uniform variable representing the time step for the simulation.
- The shader updates each particle's position based on its velocity and the elapsed time.

Step 2: Compiling the Shader to SPIR-V

COMPILE THE SHADER using glslangValidator:

```
glslangValidator -V particle_simulation.glsl -o particle_simulation.spv
```

This generates a SPIR-V binary particle_simulation.spv.

Step 3: Creating the Shader Module

CREATE A SHADER MODULE from the compiled SPIR-V:

```
VkShaderModule createShaderModule(const std::vector<char>& code) {

VkShaderModuleCreateInfo createInfo = {};

createInfo.sType = VK_STRUCTURE_TYPE_SHADER_MODULE_CREATE_INFO;

createInfo.codeSize = code.size();

createInfo.pCode = reinterpret_cast<const uint32_t*>(code.data());

VkShaderModule shaderModule;

if (vkCreateShaderModule(device, &createInfo, nullptr, &shaderModule) != VK_SUCCESS) {

throw std::runtime_error("Failed to create shader module!");

}

return shaderModule;

}

auto computeShaderCode = readFile("particle_simulation.spv");

VkShaderModule computeShaderModule = createShaderModule(computeShaderCode);
```

Step 4: Setting Up the Compute Pipeline

SET UP THE COMPUTE pipeline using the shader module:

```
VkPipelineShaderStageCreateInfo shaderStageInfo = {};

shaderStageInfo.sType =
VK_STRUCTURE_TYPE_PIPELINE_SHADER_STAGE_CREATE_

shaderStageInfo.stage =
VK_SHADER_STAGE_COMPUTE_BIT;

shaderStageInfo.module = computeShaderModule;

shaderStageInfo.pName = "main";

VkComputePipelineCreateInfo pipelineInfo = {};

pipelineInfo.sType =
VK_STRUCTURE_TYPE_COMPUTE_PIPELINE_CREATE_INFC

pipelineInfo.stage = shaderStageInfo;

pipelineInfo.layout = pipelineLayout; // Previously created pipeline
layout with descriptor sets

VkPipeline computePipeline;

if (vkCreateComputePipelines(device, VK_NULL_HANDLE, 1,
&pipelineInfo, nullptr, &computePipeline) != VK_SUCCESS) {

throw std::runtime_error("Failed to create compute pipeline!");

}
```

Dispatching the Compute Shader

TO EXECUTE THE COMPUTE shader, use a dispatch command specifying the number of workgroups:

```
vkCmdBindPipeline(commandBuffer,
VK_PIPELINE_BIND_POINT_COMPUTE,
computePipeline);

vkCmdBindDescriptorSets(commandBuffer,
VK_PIPELINE_BIND_POINT_COMPUTE, pipelineLayout, 0,
1, &descriptorSet, 0, nullptr);

uint32_t numParticles = 1024;

vkCmdDispatch(commandBuffer, (numParticles + 255) / 256, 1,
1);
```

In this example:

- numParticles is the total number of particles to simulate.
- We calculate the number of workgroups as (numParticles + 255) / 256 to ensure all particles are covered.

Synchronization Between Compute and Graphics Pipelines

WHEN OFFLOADING TASKS to the compute pipeline, you often need to synchronize data between the compute and graphics stages. For example, if you update particle positions in a compute shader and then render the particles in the graphics pipeline, you must ensure the compute shader completes before rendering begins.

Use pipeline barriers to synchronize:

```
VkBufferMemoryBarrier bufferBarrier = {};

bufferBarrier.sType = VK_STRUCTURE_TYPE_BUFFER_MEMORY_BARRIER;

bufferBarrier.srcAccessMask = VK_ACCESS_SHADER_WRITE_BIT;

bufferBarrier.dstAccessMask = VK_ACCESS_VERTEX_ATTRIBUTE_READ_BIT;

bufferBarrier.srcQueueFamilyIndex = VK_QUEUE_FAMILY_IGNORED;

bufferBarrier.dstQueueFamilyIndex = VK_QUEUE_FAMILY_IGNORED;

bufferBarrier.buffer = particleBuffer;

bufferBarrier.offset = 0;

bufferBarrier.size = VK_WHOLE_SIZE;

vkCmdPipelineBarrier(

commandBuffer,

VK_PIPELINE_STAGE_COMPUTE_SHADER_BIT,

VK_PIPELINE_STAGE_VERTEX_INPUT_BIT,

0,

0, nullptr,

1, &bufferBarrier,
```

```
0, nullptr
);
```

This barrier ensures that the particle buffer written by the compute shader is visible to the vertex shader in the graphics pipeline.

Optimizing Compute Workloads

Choosing Workgroup Sizes

SELECTING THE RIGHT workgroup size is crucial for performance. Workgroup sizes should align with the GPU's hardware capabilities:

- **NVIDIA GPUs** typically have 32 threads per warp. A workgroup size of 256 or 512 is often optimal.
- **AMD GPUs** use wavefronts of 64 threads. Workgroup sizes that are multiples of 64 work well.

Minimizing Memory Transfers

MINIMIZE DATA TRANSFERS between the CPU and GPU to reduce latency. Use GPU-only buffers for frequent computations and update them on the GPU side using compute shaders.

Using Shared Memory

SHARED MEMORY WITHIN a workgroup allows threads to collaborate and share data efficiently. This can reduce the need for global memory access, improving performance.

Example of using shared memory in a compute shader:

```
#version 450

layout(local_size_x = 256) in;

shared float sharedData[256];

layout(set = 0, binding = 0) buffer Input {

float data[];

};

void main() {

uint idx = gl_LocalInvocationID.x;

sharedData[idx] = data[idx];

barrier(); // Ensure all threads write to shared memory before proceeding

// Perform computation using sharedData

sharedData[idx] *= 2.0;

data[idx] = sharedData[idx];

}
```

Conclusion

OFFLOADING WORKLOADS to compute pipelines in Vulkan can significantly improve performance by leveraging the parallel processing power of GPUs. By effectively using compute shaders, synchronization, and optimization techniques, you can distribute complex tasks across the GPU and reduce bottlenecks in graphics rendering. Compute pipelines are versatile tools that unlock the potential for high-performance simulations, image processing, and AI computations in real-time applications.

Real-World Applications of Compute Shaders

COMPUTE SHADERS PROVIDE a versatile and powerful way to leverage the GPU for tasks that go beyond traditional graphics rendering. They allow developers to perform highly parallel computations directly on the GPU, making them ideal for real-world applications in areas such as physics simulations, particle systems, artificial intelligence, image processing, and scientific computing. This section explores several real-world use cases for compute shaders, complete with examples, considerations, and optimization strategies.

1. Physics Simulations

COMPUTE SHADERS ARE widely used to simulate physical systems due to their ability to process large amounts of data concurrently. Common applications include fluid dynamics, rigid body simulations, soft body dynamics, and cloth simulation.

Example: Particle Simulation with Gravity

IN THIS EXAMPLE, WE simulate particles influenced by gravity. Each particle has a position and velocity that are updated over time based on gravitational acceleration.

Compute Shader Code (GLSL):

```
#version 450

layout(local_size_x = 256) in;
```

```
struct Particle {
vec2 position;
vec2 velocity;
};
layout(set = 0, binding = 0) buffer Particles {
Particle particles[];
};
uniform float deltaTime;
const vec2 gravity = vec2(0.0, -9.81);
void main() {
uint idx = gl_GlobalInvocationID.x;
particles[idx].velocity += gravity * deltaTime;
particles[idx].position += particles[idx].velocity * deltaTime;
}
```

Explanation:

1. **deltaTime**: The time step for the simulation.
2. **Gravity**: A constant acceleration acting downward.
3. **Update Rules**: Each particle's velocity is updated by adding the effect of gravity, and the position is updated based on the new velocity.

Dispatch Call:

```
uint32_t numParticles = 1024;
vkCmdDispatch(commandBuffer, (numParticles + 255) / 256, 1, 1);
```

Optimization Tips:

- **Use Shared Memory**: For interactions between particles, use shared memory to reduce global memory access.
- **Double Buffering**: Maintain two buffers (current and next state) to avoid race conditions during updates.
- **Reduce Synchronization**: Minimize the use of barriers to improve performance.

---

2. Image Processing

COMPUTE SHADERS CAN efficiently handle image processing tasks, such as filtering, edge detection, Gaussian blurring, and HDR tone mapping. These tasks benefit from the parallel nature of GPUs, enabling real-time image manipulation.

Example: Gaussian Blur

GAUSSIAN BLUR IS USED to smooth images by averaging the color of neighboring pixels. This is often implemented in two passes: a horizontal blur followed by a vertical blur.

Horizontal Blur Compute Shader:

```
#version 450
```

```
layout(local_size_x = 16, local_size_y = 16) in;

layout(set = 0, binding = 0) uniform sampler2D inputImage;

layout(set = 0, binding = 1, rgba8) uniform writeonly image2D outputImage;

const float weights[5] = float[](0.227, 0.194, 0.121, 0.054, 0.016);

void main() {

ivec2 pos = ivec2(gl_GlobalInvocationID.xy);

vec3 color = texelFetch(inputImage, pos, 0).rgb * weights[0];

for (int i = 1; i < 5; i++) {

color += texelFetch(inputImage, pos + ivec2(i, 0), 0).rgb * weights[i];

color += texelFetch(inputImage, pos - ivec2(i, 0), 0).rgb * weights[i];

}

imageStore(outputImage, pos, vec4(color, 1.0));

}
```

Vertical Blur Compute Shader:

```
#version 450

layout(local_size_x = 16, local_size_y = 16) in;

layout(set = 0, binding = 0) uniform sampler2D inputImage;

layout(set = 0, binding = 1, rgba8) uniform writeonly image2D outputImage;
```

```
const float weights[5] = float[](0.227, 0.194, 0.121, 0.054, 0.016);

void main() {

ivec2 pos = ivec2(gl_GlobalInvocationID.xy);

vec3 color = texelFetch(inputImage, pos, 0).rgb * weights[0];

for (int i = 1; i < 5; i++) {

color += texelFetch(inputImage, pos + ivec2(0, i), 0).rgb * weights[i];

color += texelFetch(inputImage, pos - ivec2(0, i), 0).rgb * weights[i];

}

imageStore(outputImage, pos, vec4(color, 1.0));

}
```

Dispatch Call:

```
vkCmdDispatch(commandBuffer, (imageWidth + 15) / 16, (imageHeight + 15) / 16, 1);
```

Optimization Tips:

- **Use Local Workgroups**: Divide the image into smaller tiles to exploit locality.
- **Ping-Pong Buffers**: Alternate between two buffers for successive passes.
- **Vectorized Operations**: Use vec4 operations to process multiple color channels simultaneously.

3. Artificial Intelligence (AI) and Neural Networks

COMPUTE SHADERS CAN accelerate inference tasks in machine learning applications by performing parallel computations on large datasets. They are used for tasks such as image classification, object detection, and natural language processing.

Example: Simple Neural Network Inference

CONSIDER A FULLY CONNECTED layer in a neural network:

Compute Shader Code:

```
#version 450

layout(local_size_x = 256) in;

layout(set = 0, binding = 0) buffer Input {

float input[];

};

layout(set = 0, binding = 1) buffer Weights {

float weights[];

};

layout(set = 0, binding = 2) buffer Output {

float output[];

};

uniform uint inputSize;

uniform uint outputSize;
```

```
void main() {
uint idx = gl_GlobalInvocationID.x;
if (idx >= outputSize) return;
float sum = 0.0;
for (uint i = 0; i < inputSize; i++) {
sum += input[i] * weights[idx * inputSize + i];
}
output[idx] = sum;
}
```

Dispatch Call:

```
uint32_t outputSize = 512;
vkCmdDispatch(commandBuffer, (outputSize + 255) / 256, 1, 1);
```

Optimization Tips:

- **Batch Processing**: Process multiple inputs in a single dispatch call.
- **Quantization**: Use lower precision (e.g., float16) to speed up computation.
- **Shared Memory**: Store weights in shared memory to reduce memory latency.

4. Scientific Computing

COMPUTE SHADERS ARE ideal for simulations in fields such as physics, chemistry, and biology. Examples include molecular dynamics, fluid simulations, and finite element analysis.

Example: Heat Diffusion Simulation

COMPUTE SHADER CODE:

```
#version 450

layout(local_size_x = 16, local_size_y = 16) in;

layout(set = 0, binding = 0, r32f) uniform image2D inputImage;

layout(set = 0, binding = 1, r32f) uniform writeonly image2D outputImage;

void main() {

ivec2 pos = ivec2(gl_GlobalInvocationID.xy);

float center = imageLoad(inputImage, pos).r;

float left = imageLoad(inputImage, pos + ivec2(-1, 0)).r;

float right = imageLoad(inputImage, pos + ivec2(1, 0)).r;

float up = imageLoad(inputImage, pos + ivec2(0, 1)).r;

float down = imageLoad(inputImage, pos + ivec2(0, -1)).r;

float newTemp = center + 0.1 * (left + right + up + down - 4.0 * center);

imageStore(outputImage, pos, vec4(newTemp));
```

```
}
```

Conclusion

COMPUTE SHADERS IN Vulkan offer a versatile and powerful way to accelerate a wide range of real-world applications. From physics simulations to image processing, AI inference, and scientific computing, compute shaders harness the GPU's parallel processing capabilities to achieve high performance. By understanding the principles of compute pipelines, workgroups, and synchronization, developers can create efficient and scalable applications that fully leverage modern hardware.

Chapter 8: Debugging and Optimization

Using Vulkan Validation Layers

DEBUGGING GRAPHICS applications in Vulkan can be more challenging than in traditional graphics APIs like OpenGL or DirectX due to its explicit nature. Vulkan gives developers fine-grained control over hardware, but this control comes at the cost of increased complexity. Errors in resource management, synchronization, or command buffer execution can lead to subtle issues that are difficult to diagnose. Fortunately, Vulkan provides a powerful debugging tool called *validation layers* to help identify potential problems early in the development process.

Validation layers are optional components that hook into the Vulkan API call stream and validate each call according to the Vulkan specification. They help catch issues like incorrect API usage, resource leaks, and synchronization errors. In this section, we will explore how to use Vulkan validation layers effectively, set them up, and interpret their outputs.

Enabling Validation Layers

TO USE VALIDATION LAYERS in your Vulkan application, you must first enable them during instance creation. The validation layers are included as part of the *LunarG Vulkan SDK*, making it straightforward to integrate them into your project.

When creating a VkInstance, you can specify which layers to enable. Here's an example of how to enable the standard validation layer:

```
const char* validationLayers[] = {
```

```
"VK_LAYER_KHRONOS_validation"
};
VkInstanceCreateInfo createInfo = {};
createInfo.sType = VK_STRUCTURE_TYPE_INSTANCE_CREATE_INFO;
createInfo.enabledLayerCount = 1;
createInfo.ppEnabledLayerNames = validationLayers;
VkInstance instance;
if (vkCreateInstance(&createInfo, nullptr, &instance) != VK_SUCCESS) {
throw std::runtime_error("Failed to create Vulkan instance with validation layers!");
}
```

The "VK_LAYER_KHRONOS_validation" layer is a comprehensive validation layer provided by Khronos. It consolidates multiple validation layers into a single, easy-to-use layer.

Checking for Layer Support

BEFORE ENABLING VALIDATION layers, it's a good practice to check if they are supported on the system. Here's how you can do this:

```
bool checkValidationLayerSupport() {
uint32_t layerCount;
```

```
vkEnumerateInstanceLayerProperties(&layerCount, nullptr);

std::vector<VkLayerProperties> availableLayers(layerCount);

vkEnumerateInstanceLayerProperties(&layerCount,
availableLayers.data());

for (const char* layerName : validationLayers) {

bool layerFound = false;

for (const auto& layerProperties : availableLayers) {

if (strcmp(layerName, layerProperties.layerName) == 0) {

layerFound = true;

break;

}

}

if (!layerFound) {

return false;

}

}

return true;

}
```

Call this function before creating the VkInstance to ensure that the validation layers are available. If they are not, you can gracefully handle the error or proceed without them.

Setting Up Debug Callback

TO RECEIVE DETAILED error messages and warnings from the validation layers, you need to set up a debug callback. Vulkan provides the VkDebugUtilsMessengerEXT structure for this purpose.

Here's an example of setting up a debug callback:

```
VkDebugUtilsMessengerEXT debugMessenger;

VkDebugUtilsMessengerCreateInfoEXT debugCreateInfo = {};

debugCreateInfo.sType =
VK_STRUCTURE_TYPE_DEBUG_UTILS_MESSENGER_CREAT

debugCreateInfo.messageSeverity =

VK_DEBUG_UTILS_MESSAGE_SEVERITY_VERBOSE_BIT_EXT
|

VK_DEBUG_UTILS_MESSAGE_SEVERITY_WARNING_BIT_EXT
|

VK_DEBUG_UTILS_MESSAGE_SEVERITY_ERROR_BIT_EXT;

debugCreateInfo.messageType =

VK_DEBUG_UTILS_MESSAGE_TYPE_GENERAL_BIT_EXT
|

VK_DEBUG_UTILS_MESSAGE_TYPE_VALIDATION_BIT_EXT
|

VK_DEBUG_UTILS_MESSAGE_TYPE_PERFORMANCE_BIT_EX

debugCreateInfo.pfnUserCallback = debugCallback;
```

```
if (CreateDebugUtilsMessengerEXT(instance, &debugCreateInfo, nullptr, &debugMessenger) != VK_SUCCESS) {

throw std::runtime_error("Failed to set up debug messenger!");

}
```

The debugCallback function handles the messages from the validation layers:

```
VKAPI_ATTR VkBool32 VKAPI_CALL debugCallback(

VkDebugUtilsMessageSeverityFlagBitsEXT messageSeverity,

VkDebugUtilsMessageTypeFlagsEXT messageType,

const VkDebugUtilsMessengerCallbackDataEXT* pCallbackData,

void* pUserData) {

std::cerr << "Validation Layer: " << pCallbackData->pMessage << std::endl;

return VK_FALSE;

}
```

Destroying the Debug Messenger

DON'T FORGET TO CLEAN up the debug messenger when you destroy the Vulkan instance:

```
void DestroyDebugUtilsMessengerEXT(VkInstance instance, VkDebugUtilsMessengerEXT debugMessenger, const VkAllocationCallbacks* pAllocator) {
```

```
auto func = (PFN_vkDestroyDebugUtilsMessengerEXT)vkGetInstanceProcAddr(insta
"vkDestroyDebugUtilsMessengerEXT");

if (func != nullptr) {

func(instance, debugMessenger, pAllocator);

}

}

// In the cleanup function:

DestroyDebugUtilsMessengerEXT(instance, debugMessenger, nullptr);
```

Types of Validation Messages

VALIDATION LAYERS PROVIDE different types of messages categorized by severity and type:

1. **Message Severities:**

   ○ **VK_DEBUG_UTILS_MESSAGE_SEVERITY_VERBOSE_BIT_** Informational messages, useful for debugging purposes.

   ○ **VK_DEBUG_UTILS_MESSAGE_SEVERITY_WARNING_BIT** Warnings indicating potential issues that may not cause immediate failures.

   ○ **VK_DEBUG_UTILS_MESSAGE_SEVERITY_ERROR_BIT_E** Errors indicating invalid usage or potential crashes.

2. **Message Types:**

- ○ **VK_DEBUG_UTILS_MESSAGE_TYPE_GENERAL_BIT_E** General information that does not fit other categories.
- ○ **VK_DEBUG_UTILS_MESSAGE_TYPE_VALIDATION_BIT** Issues related to invalid Vulkan API usage.
- ○ **VK_DEBUG_UTILS_MESSAGE_TYPE_PERFORMANCE_** Warnings related to potential performance issues.

Common Validation Errors and Their Solutions

1. Invalid Command Buffer Usage

ERROR EXAMPLE:

VUID-vkQueueSubmit-pCommandBuffers-00072: Command buffer submitted multiple times without `VK_COMMAND_BUFFER_USAGE_ONE_TIME_SUBMIT_BIT

Solution:

When recording a command buffer meant for single use, set the usage flag accordingly:

VkCommandBufferBeginInfo beginInfo = {};

beginInfo.sType = VK_STRUCTURE_TYPE_COMMAND_BUFFER_BEGIN_INFO beginInfo.flags = VK_COMMAND_BUFFER_USAGE_ONE_TIME_SUBMIT_BIT;

2. Synchronization Issues

ERROR EXAMPLE:

VUID-vkQueueSubmit-pWaitSemaphores-00069: Semaphore wait not properly synchronized with command buffer execution.

Solution:

Ensure that semaphores are correctly signaled before waiting on them and that they match the correct stages in the pipeline:

```
VkSubmitInfo submitInfo = {};

submitInfo.sType = VK_STRUCTURE_TYPE_SUBMIT_INFO;

submitInfo.waitSemaphoreCount = 1;

submitInfo.pWaitSemaphores = &imageAvailableSemaphore;

VkPipelineStageFlags waitStages[] = { VK_PIPELINE_STAGE_COLOR_ATTACHMENT_OUTPUT_BIT };

submitInfo.pWaitDstStageMask = waitStages;
```

3. Memory Leaks

ERROR EXAMPLE:

Object leak detected: VkImage not destroyed before instance destruction.

Solution:

Ensure proper cleanup of Vulkan resources:

```
vkDestroyImage(device, image, nullptr);
```

Best Practices for Debugging

1. **Enable Validation Layers Early**: Use validation layers from the start of development to catch errors early.
2. **Use Debug Markers**: For more informative messages, use debug markers to label Vulkan objects.
3. **Log Messages**: Log validation messages to a file for detailed analysis.
4. **Iterative Development**: Test code changes incrementally to isolate issues.
5. **Disable Validation in Production**: Remove validation layers in release builds for better performance.

BY EFFECTIVELY USING Vulkan validation layers, you can streamline debugging, reduce development time, and ensure your application conforms to best practices.

Profiling and Performance Analysis

OPTIMIZING A VULKAN application involves identifying bottlenecks and ensuring efficient use of hardware resources. Unlike traditional graphics APIs, Vulkan's explicit control over resources and synchronization means that developers have more opportunities to optimize but also more potential pitfalls. Profiling and performance analysis are essential steps to achieve high-performance rendering and compute operations.

In this section, we will explore various techniques, tools, and best practices for profiling and analyzing Vulkan applications. We will cover GPU profiling, CPU profiling, synchronization analysis, and common performance pitfalls along with solutions.

Understanding Vulkan Performance Bottlenecks

PERFORMANCE BOTTLENECKS in Vulkan applications can broadly be categorized into two types:

1. **GPU Bottlenecks**:

   ○ **Shader Execution**: Inefficient shader code or complex computations.

   ○ **Memory Bandwidth**: Excessive data transfers between CPU and GPU.

   ○ **Pipeline Stalls**: Delays in pipeline stages due to resource dependencies.

2. **CPU Bottlenecks**:

   ○ **Command Buffer Submission**: Overhead in preparing and submitting command buffers.

   ○ **Synchronization Overhead**: Excessive or improper use of fences and semaphores.

   ○ **Resource Management**: Inefficient allocation and deallocation of resources.

Identifying whether the bottleneck lies on the CPU or GPU helps determine the appropriate optimization strategy.

Tools for Vulkan Profiling

SEVERAL TOOLS ARE AVAILABLE for profiling Vulkan applications. These tools provide insights into GPU and CPU performance, helping identify bottlenecks and inefficient code paths.

1. RenderDoc

RENDERDOC IS A POWERFUL, open-source graphics debugger that supports Vulkan. It captures frame snapshots and allows you to inspect draw calls, resources, and pipeline states.

Key Features:

- **Frame Capture**: Capture a single frame and analyze each draw call.
- **Resource Inspection**: View textures, buffers, and their contents.
- **Pipeline State**: Inspect pipeline configurations and shader inputs.

Using RenderDoc:

1. Launch your Vulkan application through RenderDoc.
2. Press the capture hotkey (default: F12) to capture a frame.
3. Analyze the captured frame to identify issues with draw calls, shader execution, and resource usage.

2. NVIDIA Nsight Graphics

NVIDIA NSIGHT GRAPHICS is a comprehensive GPU profiling tool that supports Vulkan. It provides detailed performance metrics and debugging capabilities.

Key Features:

- **Frame Debugging**: Step through draw calls and inspect GPU state.
- **Performance Counters**: Monitor GPU utilization, shader execution times, and memory usage.
- **Pipeline Viewer**: Visualize the entire pipeline and identify bottlenecks.

Using Nsight Graphics:

1. Launch Nsight Graphics and attach it to your Vulkan application.
2. Capture a frame and view performance metrics.
3. Use the pipeline viewer to analyze shader execution and resource dependencies.

3. AMD Radeon GPU Profiler (RGP)

RGP IS A PERFORMANCE profiling tool for AMD GPUs that supports Vulkan applications. It provides detailed analysis of GPU workloads.

Key Features:

- **GPU Workload Graphs**: Visualize GPU command execution over time.

- **Shader Analysis**: Inspect shader performance and resource usage.

- **Wavefront Analysis**: Analyze shader wavefront occupancy and execution efficiency.

Using RGP:

1. Launch your Vulkan application with RGP enabled.
2. Capture a profiling session and analyze the workload graphs.
3. Identify shader hotspots and optimize accordingly.

4. Intel Graphics Performance Analyzers (GPA)

INTEL GPA OFFERS A suite of tools for profiling and optimizing Vulkan applications on Intel GPUs.

Key Features:

- **Real-Time Metrics**: Monitor frame rates, GPU usage, and memory bandwidth.

- **Frame Analyzer**: Inspect individual frames and draw calls.

- **System Analyzer**: Profile CPU and GPU performance in real-time.

Using Intel GPA:

1. Launch GPA and run your Vulkan application.

2. Capture frames and view performance metrics.
3. Identify bottlenecks using the frame and system analyzers.

CPU Profiling in Vulkan Applications

EFFICIENT CPU USAGE is critical for maintaining high frame rates in Vulkan applications. CPU profiling tools help identify slow code paths, excessive memory allocations, and synchronization issues.

Tools for CPU Profiling

- **Visual Studio Profiler**: Integrated CPU profiler for Windows applications.
- **Perf (Linux)**: Command-line performance profiling tool for Linux.
- **Instruments (macOS)**: Part of Xcode for profiling macOS applications.
- **Tracy**: Real-time, frame-by-frame profiler for C++ applications.

EXAMPLE WORKFLOW WITH **Visual Studio Profiler**:

1. **Launch Profiler**: Open your project in Visual Studio and go to **Debug > Performance Profiler**.
2. **Start Profiling**: Run your application under the profiler.
3. **Analyze Results**: Identify functions with high CPU usage, excessive allocations, or long execution times.

Optimizing Command Buffer Submission

ONE COMMON CPU BOTTLENECK in Vulkan is command buffer submission. To optimize this process:

Reuse Command Buffers: Allocate command buffers once and reset them instead of creating new ones.

cpp

```
vkResetCommandBuffer(commandBuffer, 0);
```

1.

2. **Multi-Threaded Command Recording**: Record command buffers in parallel using multiple threads to distribute CPU workload.

Batch Submissions: Submit multiple command buffers in a single vkQueueSubmit call to reduce driver overhead.

cpp

```
VkSubmitInfo submitInfo = {};

submitInfo.sType = VK_STRUCTURE_TYPE_SUBMIT_INFO;

submitInfo.commandBufferCount = 2;

submitInfo.pCommandBuffers = commandBuffers;

vkQueueSubmit(graphicsQueue, 1, &submitInfo, VK_NULL_HANDLE);
```

1.

GPU Profiling Techniques

PROFILING THE GPU REQUIRES analyzing various aspects of rendering, including shader execution, memory access, and pipeline efficiency.

1. Pipeline Statistics Queries

VULKAN SUPPORTS PIPELINE statistics queries to gather performance data such as the number of vertices processed, primitives rendered, and fragment shader invocations.

Example of Using Pipeline Statistics Queries:

```
VkQueryPoolCreateInfo queryPoolInfo = {};

queryPoolInfo.sType =
VK_STRUCTURE_TYPE_QUERY_POOL_CREATE_INFO;

queryPoolInfo.queryType =
VK_QUERY_TYPE_PIPELINE_STATISTICS;

queryPoolInfo.queryCount = 1;

queryPoolInfo.pipelineStatistics =
VK_QUERY_PIPELINE_STATISTIC_VERTEX_SHADER_INVOC

VkQueryPool queryPool;

vkCreateQueryPool(device, &queryPoolInfo, nullptr, &queryPool);

// Begin query

vkCmdBeginQuery(commandBuffer, queryPool, 0, 0);

// Draw call
```

```
vkCmdDraw(commandBuffer, 3, 1, 0, 0);

// End query

vkCmdEndQuery(commandBuffer, queryPool, 0);

// Retrieve results

uint64_t result;

vkGetQueryPoolResults(device, queryPool, 0, 1, sizeof(result), &result, sizeof(result), VK_QUERY_RESULT_64_BIT);

std::cout << "Vertex Shader Invocations: " << result << std::endl;
```

2. Shader Optimization

SHADERS ARE A COMMON source of GPU bottlenecks. To optimize shaders:

1. **Simplify Calculations**: Avoid complex mathematical operations where possible.
2. **Minimize Branching**: Reduce if statements and dynamic flow control.
3. **Use SPIR-V Optimizers**: Tools like **spirv-opt** can optimize SPIR-V shader code.

Example of an Optimized GLSL Shader:

```
#version 450

layout(location = 0) in vec3 inPosition;

layout(location = 1) in vec2 inTexCoord;

layout(location = 0) out vec2 fragTexCoord;
```

```
void main() {

gl_Position = vec4(inPosition, 1.0);

fragTexCoord = inTexCoord;

}
```

3. Memory Access Patterns

EFFICIENT MEMORY ACCESS is crucial for GPU performance. To optimize memory access:

1. **Use Proper Buffer Alignments**: Align buffers to GPU cache line sizes (e.g., 256 bytes).
2. **Minimize Buffer Updates**: Use persistent buffers or update buffers in batches.
3. **Texture Compression**: Use compressed texture formats (e.g., BC formats) to reduce bandwidth.

Synchronization Analysis

SYNCHRONIZATION PRIMITIVES like semaphores and fences ensure proper execution order but can introduce overhead if misused.

Common Issues:

- **Over-Synchronization**: Using too many fences or waiting too frequently.

- **Pipeline Stalls**: Improper use of barriers causing the GPU to idle.

Best Practices:

- **Minimize Waits:** Use asynchronous operations and avoid waiting on the CPU.
- **Optimize Barriers:** Use the least restrictive memory barriers.

Example of Efficient Synchronization:

```
VkPipelineStageFlags waitStages[] = {
VK_PIPELINE_STAGE_COLOR_ATTACHMENT_OUTPUT_BI
};

submitInfo.pWaitDstStageMask = waitStages;
```

By employing these profiling and performance analysis techniques, you can identify bottlenecks, optimize both CPU and GPU workloads, and ensure that your Vulkan application runs efficiently.

Common Bottlenecks and Their Solutions

VULKAN'S LOW-LEVEL control over the graphics hardware offers unmatched power and flexibility, but it also increases the likelihood of encountering bottlenecks. These bottlenecks can occur due to inefficiencies in CPU usage, GPU operations, synchronization, or resource management. This section explores the most common bottlenecks encountered in Vulkan applications and provides practical solutions to address them. We will categorize these bottlenecks and discuss best practices, code examples, and strategies to mitigate them effectively.

CPU Bottlenecks

CPU BOTTLENECKS OCCUR when the CPU is unable to keep up with the GPU, resulting in under-utilization of GPU resources. This is often caused by inefficient command buffer generation, excessive draw calls, or poor multi-threading.

1. Inefficient Command Buffer Recording

PROBLEM:

Recording command buffers on the main thread can cause significant delays, especially if there are many objects or complex scenes.

Solution:

Record command buffers in parallel using multiple threads. Vulkan's thread-safe design allows command buffers to be recorded concurrently.

Example of Multi-Threaded Command Buffer Recording:

```
std::vector<std::thread> threads;

std::vector<VkCommandBuffer> commandBuffers(threadCount);

for (size_t i = 0; i < threadCount; i++) {

threads.emplace_back([&, i]() {

VkCommandBufferAllocateInfo allocInfo = {};

allocInfo.sType =
VK_STRUCTURE_TYPE_COMMAND_BUFFER_ALLOCATE_INF

allocInfo.commandPool = commandPool;
```

```
allocInfo.level                                                  =
VK_COMMAND_BUFFER_LEVEL_SECONDARY;

allocInfo.commandBufferCount = 1;

vkAllocateCommandBuffers(device,                         &allocInfo,
&commandBuffers[i]);

VkCommandBufferBeginInfo beginInfo = {};

beginInfo.sType                                                  =
VK_STRUCTURE_TYPE_COMMAND_BUFFER_BEGIN_INFO;

beginInfo.flags                                                  =
VK_COMMAND_BUFFER_USAGE_RENDER_PASS_CONTINU

vkBeginCommandBuffer(commandBuffers[i], &beginInfo);

// Record commands here

vkEndCommandBuffer(commandBuffers[i]);

});

}

for (auto& thread : threads) {

thread.join();

}
```

2. Excessive Draw Calls

PROBLEM:

Submitting too many small draw calls can overwhelm the CPU and the driver, leading to significant overhead.

Solution:

Batch draw calls where possible by combining multiple objects into a single vertex buffer and using *instanced rendering*.

Example of Instanced Rendering:

vkCmdDraw(commandBuffer, vertexCount, instanceCount, firstVertex, firstInstance);

This reduces the number of draw calls and leverages GPU capabilities to draw multiple instances of an object efficiently.

3. Resource Allocation Overhead

PROBLEM:

Frequent allocation and deallocation of buffers and images can cause memory fragmentation and performance degradation.

Solution:

Use a resource allocator like **Vulkan Memory Allocator (VMA)** to manage memory efficiently and avoid frequent allocations.

Example of Using VMA:

VmaAllocatorCreateInfo allocatorInfo = {};

allocatorInfo.physicalDevice = physicalDevice;

allocatorInfo.device = device;

allocatorInfo.instance = instance;

VmaAllocator allocator;

vmaCreateAllocator(&allocatorInfo, &allocator);

```
// Allocate a buffer

VmaAllocationCreateInfo allocCreateInfo = {};

allocCreateInfo.usage =
VMA_MEMORY_USAGE_GPU_ONLY;

VkBufferCreateInfo bufferInfo = {};

bufferInfo.sType =
VK_STRUCTURE_TYPE_BUFFER_CREATE_INFO;

bufferInfo.size = bufferSize;

bufferInfo.usage =
VK_BUFFER_USAGE_VERTEX_BUFFER_BIT;

VkBuffer buffer;

VmaAllocation allocation;

vmaCreateBuffer(allocator, &bufferInfo, &allocCreateInfo,
&buffer, &allocation, nullptr);
```

GPU Bottlenecks

GPU BOTTLENECKS OCCUR when the graphics hardware is the limiting factor, often due to inefficient shader code, poor memory access patterns, or high rendering complexity.

1. Shader Complexity

PROBLEM:

Overly complex shaders with expensive calculations can slow down rendering significantly.

Solution:

- **Simplify Shader Logic**: Avoid complex mathematical functions where possible.
- **Precompute Values**: Move calculations to the CPU if they can be done once and passed as uniforms.
- **Use SPIR-V Optimizers**: Tools like spirv-opt can optimize shader bytecode.

Example of Simplified GLSL Shader:

```
#version 450

layout(location = 0) in vec3 inPosition;

layout(location = 1) in vec3 inNormal;

layout(location = 0) out vec4 outColor;

layout(set = 0, binding = 0) uniform UBO {

mat4 modelViewProjection;

vec3 lightDir;

} ubo;

void main() {

float intensity = max(dot(normalize(inNormal), ubo.lightDir), 0.0);

outColor = vec4(vec3(intensity), 1.0);

gl_Position = ubo.modelViewProjection * vec4(inPosition, 1.0);
```

```
}
```

2. Memory Bandwidth Issues

PROBLEM:

Excessive or inefficient memory access patterns can lead to GPU stalls and reduced performance.

Solution:

- **Use Texture Compression**: Use formats like BC1/BC3 to reduce texture size.
- **Optimize Buffer Layout**: Align buffers to the GPU cache line size (typically 256 bytes).
- **Minimize Data Transfers**: Use *staging buffers* to upload data in bulk rather than frequent small uploads.

3. Fragment Shader Overdraw

PROBLEM:

Rendering the same pixels multiple times due to overlapping geometry can lead to unnecessary fragment shader invocations.

Solution:

- **Depth Pre-Pass**: Render the scene's depth information first to avoid processing hidden fragments.
- **Frustum Culling**: Exclude objects outside the camera's view.

- **Occlusion Culling**: Skip rendering objects that are occluded by other geometry.

Example of Depth Pre-Pass:

```
vkCmdBindPipeline(commandBuffer,
VK_PIPELINE_BIND_POINT_GRAPHICS,
depthPrePassPipeline);

vkCmdDraw(commandBuffer, vertexCount, 1, 0, 0);

// Later render pass skips hidden fragments

vkCmdBindPipeline(commandBuffer,
VK_PIPELINE_BIND_POINT_GRAPHICS, mainPipeline);

vkCmdDraw(commandBuffer, vertexCount, 1, 0, 0);
```

Synchronization Bottlenecks

IMPROPER SYNCHRONIZATION can cause the CPU or GPU to stall, reducing overall performance.

1. Over-Synchronization

PROBLEM:

Using too many fences or waiting on the GPU frequently can cause the CPU to idle unnecessarily.

Solution:

Use *asynchronous execution* and minimize blocking waits.

Example of Non-Blocking Fence Check:

```
VkResult result = vkGetFenceStatus(device, fence);
```

```
if (result == VK_SUCCESS) {

// Fence signaled, proceed

} else {

// Fence not signaled, perform other tasks

}
```

2. Pipeline Barriers

PROBLEM:

Unnecessary or overly strict pipeline barriers can stall the GPU.

Solution:

Use the least restrictive barriers possible and only insert them where resource hazards exist.

Example of Optimized Pipeline Barrier:

```
VkImageMemoryBarrier barrier = {};

barrier.sType =
VK_STRUCTURE_TYPE_IMAGE_MEMORY_BARRIER;

barrier.oldLayout = VK_IMAGE_LAYOUT_UNDEFINED;

barrier.newLayout =
VK_IMAGE_LAYOUT_COLOR_ATTACHMENT_OPTIMAL;

barrier.srcAccessMask = 0;

barrier.dstAccessMask =
VK_ACCESS_COLOR_ATTACHMENT_WRITE_BIT;
```

```
barrier.srcStageMask =
VK_PIPELINE_STAGE_TOP_OF_PIPE_BIT;

barrier.dstStageMask =
VK_PIPELINE_STAGE_COLOR_ATTACHMENT_OUTPUT_BIT;

vkCmdPipelineBarrier(commandBuffer,

VK_PIPELINE_STAGE_TOP_OF_PIPE_BIT,
VK_PIPELINE_STAGE_COLOR_ATTACHMENT_OUTPUT_BIT,

0, 0, nullptr, 0, nullptr, 1, &barrier);
```

Conclusion

UNDERSTANDING AND RESOLVING bottlenecks in Vulkan applications require a methodical approach to profiling and optimization. By addressing CPU inefficiencies, optimizing GPU workloads, and managing synchronization carefully, you can significantly enhance the performance of your application. Use the tools and techniques discussed in this section to diagnose issues and implement targeted solutions effectively.

Chapter 9: Advanced Vulkan Features

Ray Tracing with Vulkan

RAY TRACING IS A RENDERING technique that simulates the physical behavior of light to achieve photorealistic graphics. Unlike traditional rasterization, which converts 3D scenes into 2D images by projecting vertices onto a plane, ray tracing works by tracing rays from the camera through each pixel on the screen and calculating their interactions with objects in the scene. This allows for accurate simulations of effects such as reflections, refractions, shadows, and global illumination.

In Vulkan, ray tracing support was introduced through the **Vulkan Ray Tracing** extensions, namely VK_KHR_acceleration_structure, VK_KHR_ray_tracing_pipeline, and VK_KHR_ray_query. These extensions provide the necessary infrastructure to create, manage, and execute ray-traced pipelines. This section provides a detailed overview of setting up ray tracing in Vulkan, constructing acceleration structures, and implementing a basic ray-traced scene.

Prerequisites for Ray Tracing

BEFORE DIVING INTO ray tracing, ensure your environment supports the Vulkan Ray Tracing extensions. You will need:

1. **A GPU that supports ray tracing** (e.g., NVIDIA RTX or AMD RX 6000 series).
2. **Vulkan SDK** (version 1.2.162 or higher).
3. **Validation layers** for debugging ray tracing operations.
4. **Shader compiler** for GLSL and SPIR-V (e.g., glslangValidator).

Ensure the following extensions are enabled in your application:

- VK_KHR_acceleration_structure
- VK_KHR_ray_tracing_pipeline
- VK_KHR_buffer_device_address
- VK_EXT_descriptor_indexing

Creating Acceleration Structures

RAY TRACING RELIES on **acceleration structures** to speed up the process of ray traversal and intersection testing. Acceleration structures are hierarchies that spatially organize geometry to reduce the number of intersection tests per ray. Vulkan provides two types of acceleration structures:

1. **Bottom-Level Acceleration Structures (BLAS)** – Represent individual geometries.
2. **Top-Level Acceleration Structures (TLAS)** – Represent the scene by referencing BLAS instances.

Steps to Create an Acceleration Structure

DEFINE GEOMETRY DATA

Create a vertex buffer and an index buffer to represent the triangle or mesh geometry:

cpp

```
std::vector<Vertex> vertices = {

{{-0.5f, -0.5f, 0.0f}},
```

{{0.5f, -0.5f, 0.0f}},

{{0.0f, 0.5f, 0.0f}}

};

std::vector<uint32_t> indices = {0, 1, 2};

1.

Create a Bottom-Level Acceleration Structure (BLAS)

Create a VkAccelerationStructureCreateInfoKHR to define the BLAS:

cpp

VkAccelerationStructureGeometryKHR geometry = {};

geometry.sType = VK_STRUCTURE_TYPE_ACCELERATION_STRUCTURE_GEC

geometry.geometryType = VK_GEOMETRY_TYPE_TRIANGLES_KHR;

geometry.flags = VK_GEOMETRY_OPAQUE_BIT_KHR;

geometry.geometry.triangles.sType = VK_STRUCTURE_TYPE_ACCELERATION_STRUCTURE_GEC

geometry.geometry.triangles.vertexFormat = VK_FORMAT_R32G32B32_SFLOAT;

geometry.geometry.triangles.vertexData.deviceAddress = vertexBufferAddress;

geometry.geometry.triangles.indexType = VK_INDEX_TYPE_UINT32;

geometry.geometry.triangles.indexData.deviceAddress = indcxBufferAddress;

Specify build information and sizes:

cpp

VkAccelerationStructureBuildGeometryInfoKHR buildInfo = {};

buildInfo.sType = VK_STRUCTURE_TYPE_ACCELERATION_STRUCTURE_BUILI

buildInfo.type = VK_ACCELERATION_STRUCTURE_TYPE_BOTTOM_LEVEL_K

buildInfo.flags = VK_BUILD_ACCELERATION_STRUCTURE_PREFER_FAST_TRA

buildInfo.geometryCount = 1;

buildInfo.pGeometries = &geometry;

1.

Build the BLAS

Use vkCmdBuildAccelerationStructuresKHR to build the BLAS on the GPU:

cpp

vkCmdBuildAccelerationStructuresKHR(commandBuffer, 1, &buildInfo, &rangeInfo);

1.

Create a Top-Level Acceleration Structure (TLAS)

After creating the BLAS, define a TLAS that references BLAS instances:

cpp

```
VkAccelerationStructureInstanceKHR instance = {};

instance.transform = identityTransform;

instance.instanceCustomIndex = 0;

instance.mask = 0xFF;

instance.instanceShaderBindingTableRecordOffset = 0;

instance.accelerationStructureReference = blasDeviceAddress;
```

1.

Ray Tracing Pipeline

ONCE ACCELERATION STRUCTURES are set up, the next step is to create a **ray tracing pipeline**. The ray tracing pipeline in Vulkan consists of:

1. **Ray Generation Shader** – Launches rays into the scene.
2. **Closest-Hit Shader** – Executes when a ray intersects geometry.
3. **Miss Shader** – Executes when a ray does not hit any geometry.
4. **Any-Hit Shader** (optional) – Checks intersections for further processing.

Ray Generation Shader (GLSL)

#VERSION 460

#extension GL_EXT_ray_tracing : enable

layout(binding = 0, set = 0) uniform accelerationStructureEXT topLevelAS;

layout(location = 0) rayPayloadEXT vec3 payload;

void main() {

vec3 origin = vec3(0.0, 0.0, -1.0);

vec3 direction = normalize(vec3(gl_LaunchIDEXT.xy, 1.0));

traceRayEXT(topLevelAS, gl_RayFlagsOpaqueEXT, 0xFF, 0, 0, 0, origin, 0.0, direction, 1000.0, 0);

}

Closest-Hit Shader (GLSL)

#VERSION 460

#extension GL_EXT_ray_tracing : enable

layout(location = 0) rayPayloadInEXT vec3 payload;

void main() {

payload = vec3(1.0, 0.0, 0.0); // Red color for intersections

}

Miss Shader (GLSL)

#VERSION 460

#extension GL_EXT_ray_tracing : enable

```
layout(location = 0) rayPayloadInEXT vec3 payload;

void main() {

payload = vec3(0.0, 0.0, 1.0); // Blue color for missed rays

}
```

Shader Binding Table (SBT)

THE SHADER BINDING Table (SBT) maps shader records to rays. Create and bind the SBT to link ray tracing shaders:

```
VkStridedDeviceAddressRegionKHR raygenSBT = {};

raygenSBT.deviceAddress = raygenBufferAddress;

raygenSBT.stride = shaderGroupHandleSize;

raygenSBT.size = shaderGroupHandleSize;

VkStridedDeviceAddressRegionKHR missSBT = {};

missSBT.deviceAddress = missBufferAddress;

missSBT.stride = shaderGroupHandleSize;

missSBT.size = shaderGroupHandleSize;
```

Dispatching Rays

FINALLY, DISPATCH RAYS using vkCmdTraceRaysKHR:

```
vkCmdTraceRaysKHR(commandBuffer, &raygenSBT, &missSBT, &hitSBT, &callableSBT, width, height, 1);
```

Synchronization and Presentation

SYNCHRONIZE RAY TRACING commands using semaphores and submit the result to the swapchain for presentation.

Conclusion

RAY TRACING IN VULKAN provides a powerful way to achieve photorealistic graphics. By leveraging acceleration structures, ray tracing pipelines, and shader binding tables, developers can simulate complex lighting interactions with high performance. The Vulkan Ray Tracing extensions enable fine-grained control over the ray tracing process, making it suitable for games, scientific visualization, and real-time rendering applications.

Multi-Threading in Vulkan Applications

MULTI-THREADING IS essential for maximizing the performance of modern applications, especially in the context of graphics rendering. Vulkan is designed with multi-threading in mind, offering developers fine-grained control over concurrent execution of tasks such as command buffer generation, resource management, and submission to queues. Proper multi-threading can significantly improve CPU utilization, reduce frame latency, and enhance rendering throughput.

This section explores multi-threading concepts in Vulkan, strategies for parallelizing work, synchronization mechanisms, and best practices for implementing multi-threaded rendering pipelines.

Key Concepts of Multi-Threading in Vulkan

VULKAN'S ARCHITECTURE is inherently thread-safe for many operations. However, developers must manage concurrency explicitly to avoid race conditions and undefined behavior. Key concepts to understand when implementing multi-threading in Vulkan include:

1. **Thread-Safe Command Buffer Recording** – Multiple threads can record command buffers concurrently.
2. **Queue Submission** – Command buffers recorded by different threads can be submitted to queues for execution.
3. **Synchronization Primitives** – Semaphores, fences, and events manage dependencies between threads and GPU work.
4. **Pipeline Barriers** – Ensure proper memory access synchronization across different threads and GPU stages.

Strategies for Multi-Threaded Command Buffer Recording

ONE OF THE MOST EFFECTIVE ways to leverage multi-threading in Vulkan is to parallelize the recording of command buffers. Since Vulkan allows each thread to record its own command buffers independently, you can split rendering tasks among multiple threads to reduce CPU bottlenecks.

Example: Recording Command Buffers in Parallel

THE FOLLOWING EXAMPLE demonstrates how to record multiple command buffers concurrently using a thread pool.

Create Command Pools Per Thread

Each thread should have its own VkCommandPool to avoid contention:

cpp

```
std::vector<VkCommandPool> commandPools(numThreads);

for (size_t i = 0; i < numThreads; i++) {

VkCommandPoolCreateInfo poolInfo{};

poolInfo.sType = VK_STRUCTURE_TYPE_COMMAND_POOL_CREATE_INFO;

poolInfo.queueFamilyIndex = graphicsQueueFamilyIndex;

poolInfo.flags = VK_COMMAND_POOL_CREATE_RESET_COMMAND_BUFFER

vkCreateCommandPool(device, &poolInfo, nullptr, &commandPools[i]);

}
```

1.

Allocate Command Buffers

Allocate a command buffer for each thread from its respective command pool:

cpp

```
std::vector<VkCommandBuffer> commandBuffers(numThreads);

for (size_t i = 0; i < numThreads; i++) {

VkCommandBufferAllocateInfo allocInfo{};

allocInfo.sType = VK_STRUCTURE_TYPE_COMMAND_BUFFER_ALLOCATE_INF

allocInfo.commandPool = commandPools[i];
```

```
allocInfo.level = VK_COMMAND_BUFFER_LEVEL_PRIMARY;

allocInfo.commandBufferCount = 1;

vkAllocateCommandBuffers(device, &allocInfo, &commandBuffers[i]);

}
```

1.

Parallel Command Buffer Recording

Use a thread pool to record command buffers in parallel:

```cpp
std::vector<std::thread> threads;

for (size_t i = 0; i < numThreads; i++) {

threads.emplace_back([&, i]() {

VkCommandBufferBeginInfo beginInfo{};

beginInfo.sType = VK_STRUCTURE_TYPE_COMMAND_BUFFER_BEGIN_INFO;

beginInfo.flags = VK_COMMAND_BUFFER_USAGE_SIMULTANEOUS_USE_BIT

vkBeginCommandBuffer(commandBuffers[i], &beginInfo);

// Example drawing commands (replace with actual work)

vkCmdBindPipeline(commandBuffers[i], VK_PIPELINE_BIND_POINT_GRAPHICS, graphicsPipeline);
```

```
vkCmdDraw(commandBuffers[i], 3, 1, 0, 0);
vkEndCommandBuffer(commandBuffers[i]);
});
}
for (auto& thread : threads) {
thread.join();
}
```

1.

Submit Command Buffers

After recording, submit the command buffers to the graphics queue:

cpp

```
std::vector<VkSubmitInfo> submitInfos(numThreads);
for (size_t i = 0; i < numThreads; i++) {
VkSubmitInfo submitInfo{};
submitInfo.sType =
VK_STRUCTURE_TYPE_SUBMIT_INFO;
submitInfo.commandBufferCount = 1;
submitInfo.pCommandBuffers = &commandBuffers[i];
submitInfos[i] = submitInfo;
}
```

vkQueueSubmit(graphicsQueue, numThreads, submitInfos.data(), VK_NULL_HANDLE);

vkQueueWaitIdle(graphicsQueue);

1.

Synchronization Mechanisms for Multi-Threading

WHEN USING MULTIPLE threads in Vulkan, proper synchronization is critical to avoid race conditions and undefined behavior. Vulkan provides the following synchronization primitives:

1. **Fences** – Synchronize CPU with GPU work.
2. **Semaphores** – Synchronize between different GPU queues.
3. **Events** – Synchronize GPU work within the same queue.

Example: Using Fences for CPU-GPU Synchronization

FENCES CAN BE USED to ensure that CPU execution waits until GPU work completes:

VkFence fence;

VkFenceCreateInfo fenceInfo{};

fenceInfo.sType = VK_STRUCTURE_TYPE_FENCE_CREATE_INFO;

fenceInfo.flags = 0;

vkCreateFence(device, &fenceInfo, nullptr, &fence);

// Submit command buffer

VkSubmitInfo submitInfo{};

```
submitInfo.sType =
VK_STRUCTURE_TYPE_SUBMIT_INFO;

submitInfo.commandBufferCount = 1;

submitInfo.pCommandBuffers = &commandBuffer;

vkQueueSubmit(graphicsQueue, 1, &submitInfo, fence);

// Wait for the fence to signal completion

vkWaitForFences(device, 1, &fence, VK_TRUE, UINT64_MAX);

// Clean up

vkDestroyFence(device, fence, nullptr);
```

Best Practices for Multi-Threading in Vulkan

1. **Minimize Command Pool Contention** – Use separate command pools for each thread to avoid lock contention.
2. **Batch Small Draw Calls** – Group small rendering tasks together to reduce overhead from frequent submissions.
3. **Use Pipeline State Objects (PSOs) Efficiently** – Pre-create and reuse PSOs to avoid expensive state changes during rendering.
4. **Avoid Frequent Memory Allocation** – Reuse buffers and descriptor sets to minimize dynamic memory allocations.
5. **Profile and Optimize** – Use profiling tools (e.g., RenderDoc, NVIDIA Nsight) to identify CPU and GPU bottlenecks.

Multi-Threaded Resource Management

IN ADDITION TO COMMAND buffer recording, resource management can be parallelized. Tasks such as uploading textures, creating buffers, and updating descriptor sets can benefit from multi-threading. However, ensure proper synchronization when accessing shared resources.

Example: Uploading Textures in Parallel

```
STD::VECTOR<STD::THREAD> uploadThreads;

for (size_t i = 0; i < numTextures; i++) {

uploadThreads.emplace_back([&, i]() {

// Create staging buffer and copy texture data

VkBuffer stagingBuffer;

VkDeviceMemory stagingBufferMemory;

createBuffer(textureSizes[i],
VK_BUFFER_USAGE_TRANSFER_SRC_BIT,

VK_MEMORY_PROPERTY_HOST_VISIBLE_BIT |
VK_MEMORY_PROPERTY_HOST_COHERENT_BIT,

stagingBuffer, stagingBufferMemory);

void* data;

vkMapMemory(device, stagingBufferMemory, 0, textureSizes[i], 0,
&data);

memcpy(data, textureData[i], static_cast<size_t>(textureSizes[i]));

vkUnmapMemory(device, stagingBufferMemory);

// Copy staging buffer to texture image
```

```
copyBufferToImage(stagingBuffer, textureImages[i], textureWidths[i], textureHeights[i]);

vkDestroyBuffer(device, stagingBuffer, nullptr);

vkFreeMemory(device, stagingBufferMemory, nullptr);

});

}

for (auto& thread : uploadThreads) {

thread.join();

}
```

Conclusion

IMPLEMENTING MULTI-threading in Vulkan applications can significantly enhance performance by leveraging modern multi-core CPUs. Recording command buffers, managing resources, and handling queue submissions in parallel allows for efficient CPU utilization and reduces frame latency. By understanding synchronization mechanisms and adhering to best practices, developers can achieve optimal concurrency and maximize rendering throughput.

Dynamic Rendering and Adaptive Techniques

DYNAMIC RENDERING IN Vulkan represents a significant step forward for flexibility and performance in modern graphics APIs. Introduced with the VK_KHR_dynamic_rendering extension and later integrated into Vulkan 1.3, dynamic rendering allows developers to simplify and streamline their rendering workflows by eliminating the need to create and manage complex render pass objects ahead of time.

Adaptive techniques further extend dynamic rendering by enabling real-time adjustments to rendering parameters based on system performance, scene complexity, or user interactions. This combination allows for more efficient resource utilization, lower latency, and improved scalability for applications running across a wide range of hardware.

This section explores the fundamentals of dynamic rendering, its implementation in Vulkan, and adaptive techniques that can enhance rendering performance dynamically.

Overview of Dynamic Rendering

IN TRADITIONAL VULKAN, rendering requires the creation of render passes and framebuffer objects, which define how rendering will occur. Dynamic rendering allows you to bypass pre-defined render passes and framebuffers, letting you specify attachments on the fly when recording command buffers. This reduces boilerplate code and simplifies rendering pipelines.

Dynamic rendering is particularly beneficial for applications that require frequent changes to attachments, such as those employing:

- **Deferred Rendering Pipelines**
- **Forward+ and Hybrid Rendering**
- **Adaptive Resolution Scaling**
- **Multi-Viewport Rendering**

Key benefits of dynamic rendering include:

1. **Simplified API**: No need to predefine complex render passes or framebuffer configurations.
2. **Flexibility**: Attachments can be defined at recording time, allowing adaptive framebuffers and dynamic rendering techniques.
3. **Performance**: Reduces overhead from managing multiple render pass objects.

Enabling Dynamic Rendering in Vulkan

BEFORE USING DYNAMIC rendering, you need to enable the required extension and features during instance and device creation.

Enable the Extension

Add VK_KHR_dynamic_rendering to the list of device extensions:

cpp

```
const std::vector<const char*> deviceExtensions = {

VK_KHR_SWAPCHAIN_EXTENSION_NAME,

VK_KHR_DYNAMIC_RENDERING_EXTENSION_NAME

};
```

1.

Enable the Feature

When creating the Vulkan device, enable the dynamicRendering feature:

cpp

```
VkPhysicalDeviceDynamicRenderingFeatures
dynamicRenderingFeatures{};
```

```
dynamicRenderingFeatures.sType = VK_STRUCTURE_TYPE_PHYSICAL_DEVICE_DYNAMIC_REN

dynamicRenderingFeatures.dynamicRendering = VK_TRUE;

VkDeviceCreateInfo createInfo{};

createInfo.sType = VK_STRUCTURE_TYPE_DEVICE_CREATE_INFO;

createInfo.pNext = &dynamicRenderingFeatures;

createInfo.enabledExtensionCount = static_cast<uint32_t>(deviceExtensions.size());

createInfo.ppEnabledExtensionNames = deviceExtensions.data();
```

1.

Recording a Dynamic Rendering Command Buffer

DYNAMIC RENDERING REPLACES the need to define a render pass by allowing you to specify the attachments directly in the command buffer.

Begin Dynamic Rendering

Use VkRenderingInfo to specify the attachments and rendering area:

cpp

```
VkRenderingAttachmentInfo colorAttachment{};

colorAttachment.sType = VK_STRUCTURE_TYPE_RENDERING_ATTACHMENT_INFO;

colorAttachment.imageView = colorImageView;
```

colorAttachment.imageLayout = VK_IMAGE_LAYOUT_COLOR_ATTACHMENT_OPTIMAL;

colorAttachment.loadOp = VK_ATTACHMENT_LOAD_OP_CLEAR;

colorAttachment.storeOp = VK_ATTACHMENT_STORE_OP_STORE;

colorAttachment.clearValue.color = {{0.0f, 0.0f, 0.0f, 1.0f}};

VkRenderingInfo renderingInfo{};

renderingInfo.sType = VK_STRUCTURE_TYPE_RENDERING_INFO;

renderingInfo.renderArea = {{0, 0}, {width, height}};

renderingInfo.layerCount = 1;

renderingInfo.colorAttachmentCount = 1;

renderingInfo.pColorAttachments = &colorAttachment;

vkCmdBeginRendering(commandBuffer, &renderingInfo);

1.

Record Drawing Commands

After beginning dynamic rendering, record your draw commands as usual:

cpp

vkCmdBindPipeline(commandBuffer, VK_PIPELINE_BIND_POINT_GRAPHICS, graphicsPipeline);

vkCmdDraw(commandBuffer, 3, 1, 0, 0);

1.

End Dynamic Rendering

End dynamic rendering with vkCmdEndRendering:

cpp

vkCmdEndRendering(commandBuffer);

1.

Using Multiple Attachments in Dynamic Rendering

DYNAMIC RENDERING SUPPORTS multiple attachments, including color, depth, and stencil attachments. Here's an example of setting up color and depth attachments:

VkRenderingAttachmentInfo colorAttachment{};

colorAttachment.sType = VK_STRUCTURE_TYPE_RENDERING_ATTACHMENT_INFO

colorAttachment.imageView = colorImageView;

colorAttachment.imageLayout = VK_IMAGE_LAYOUT_COLOR_ATTACHMENT_OPTIMAL;

colorAttachment.loadOp = VK_ATTACHMENT_LOAD_OP_CLEAR;

colorAttachment.storeOp = VK_ATTACHMENT_STORE_OP_STORE;

colorAttachment.clearValue.color = {{0.0f, 0.0f, 0.0f, 1.0f}};

VkRenderingAttachmentInfo depthAttachment{};

depthAttachment.sType = VK_STRUCTURE_TYPE_RENDERING_ATTACHMENT_INFC

```
depthAttachment.imageView = depthImageView;

depthAttachment.imageLayout = VK_IMAGE_LAYOUT_DEPTH_STENCIL_ATTACHMENT_OPTI

depthAttachment.loadOp = VK_ATTACHMENT_LOAD_OP_CLEAR;

depthAttachment.storeOp = VK_ATTACHMENT_STORE_OP_DONT_CARE;

depthAttachment.clearValue.depthStencil = {1.0f, 0};

VkRenderingInfo renderingInfo{};

renderingInfo.sType = VK_STRUCTURE_TYPE_RENDERING_INFO;

renderingInfo.renderArea = {{0, 0}, {width, height}};

renderingInfo.layerCount = 1;

renderingInfo.colorAttachmentCount = 1;

renderingInfo.pColorAttachments = &colorAttachment;

renderingInfo.pDepthAttachment = &depthAttachment;

vkCmdBeginRendering(commandBuffer, &renderingInfo);
```

Adaptive Techniques in Dynamic Rendering

DYNAMIC RENDERING IS well-suited for implementing adaptive techniques that optimize rendering performance based on real-time conditions. Common adaptive techniques include:

1. **Adaptive Resolution Scaling**
2. **Dynamic LOD (Level of Detail) Adjustments**

3. **Variable Rate Shading (VRS)**
4. **Dynamic Quality Adjustments**

Adaptive Resolution Scaling

ADAPTIVE RESOLUTION scaling adjusts the resolution of rendered frames based on GPU load, ensuring a stable frame rate. Implementing adaptive resolution scaling involves dynamically resizing the swapchain and framebuffer attachments.

```
// Adjust resolution based on frame time

if (frameTime > targetFrameTime) {

currentWidth = std::max(minWidth, currentWidth - resolutionStep);

currentHeight = std::max(minHeight, currentHeight - resolutionStep);

} else {

currentWidth = std::min(maxWidth, currentWidth + resolutionStep);

currentHeight = std::min(maxHeight, currentHeight + resolutionStep);

}

// Recreate swapchain and framebuffers with new resolution

recreateSwapchain(currentWidth, currentHeight);
```

Dynamic LOD Adjustments

ADJUSTING THE LEVEL of detail based on the camera distance or performance metrics helps maintain performance without sacrificing visual quality.

```
float distance = glm::length(cameraPosition - objectPosition);

if (distance > lodThresholdHigh) {

useHighLOD = false;

} else {

useHighLOD = true;

}

// Bind appropriate LOD model

if (useHighLOD) {

vkCmdBindVertexBuffers(commandBuffer, 0, 1, &highLODVertexBuffer, offsets);

} else {

vkCmdBindVertexBuffers(commandBuffer, 0, 1, &lowLODVertexBuffer, offsets);

}
```

Synchronization in Dynamic Rendering

PROPER SYNCHRONIZATION ensures that dynamic rendering operations execute correctly. Use semaphores, fences, and pipeline barriers to manage dependencies.

Pipeline Barrier Example:

```
VkImageMemoryBarrier barrier{};

barrier.sType =
VK_STRUCTURE_TYPE_IMAGE_MEMORY_BARRIER;

barrier.oldLayout = VK_IMAGE_LAYOUT_UNDEFINED;

barrier.newLayout =
VK_IMAGE_LAYOUT_COLOR_ATTACHMENT_OPTIMAL;

barrier.srcAccessMask = 0;

barrier.dstAccessMask =
VK_ACCESS_COLOR_ATTACHMENT_WRITE_BIT;

barrier.image = colorImage;

barrier.subresourceRange =
{VK_IMAGE_ASPECT_COLOR_BIT, 0, 1, 0, 1};

vkCmdPipelineBarrier(

commandBuffer,

VK_PIPELINE_STAGE_TOP_OF_PIPE_BIT,

VK_PIPELINE_STAGE_COLOR_ATTACHMENT_OUTPUT_BIT

0,

0, nullptr,

0, nullptr,

1, &barrier

);
```

Conclusion

DYNAMIC RENDERING IN Vulkan offers flexibility and efficiency by removing the need for predefined render passes and framebuffers. Combined with adaptive techniques such as resolution scaling, dynamic LOD, and variable rate shading, developers can optimize rendering performance for diverse hardware and dynamic scenarios. Proper synchronization and resource management are key to leveraging these techniques effectively, resulting in scalable and high-performance graphics applications.

Chapter 10: Vulkan for Multi-Platform Development

Portability in Vulkan

IN TODAY'S DYNAMIC software landscape, creating graphics applications that run seamlessly across multiple platforms is essential. Vulkan, designed by the Khronos Group, excels at portability and multi-platform support. Unlike older graphics APIs, which were tightly coupled with specific platforms or operating systems, Vulkan provides a unified abstraction layer for modern GPUs across a wide array of devices.

This section delves into the key considerations, challenges, and strategies involved in developing Vulkan applications that are portable and efficient across different platforms. By understanding these concepts, you can leverage Vulkan's cross-platform capabilities to deliver high-performance applications across desktop, mobile, and embedded systems.

The Concept of Platform Abstraction in Vulkan

ONE OF VULKAN'S DEFINING characteristics is its platform-agnostic nature. Vulkan decouples the API's core functionality from the windowing system and platform-specific operations. This is achieved through a set of *platform-specific extensions* and the *Vulkan loader* mechanism.

- **Loader and Layers**: The Vulkan loader acts as a bridge between your application and the hardware driver. It dynamically loads the appropriate driver and manages platform-specific functions. This abstraction ensures that your code can work on Windows, Linux, macOS, and mobile operating systems without significant changes.

- **Surface Extensions**: To interface with a platform's windowing system (e.g., Win32, X11, Wayland, Metal, or Android), Vulkan uses surface extensions. These extensions provide the necessary functionality to create swapchains and manage presentation on the target platform.

For example, on Windows, you would use the VK_KHR_win32_surface extension, whereas on Linux, you might use VK_KHR_xcb_surface or VK_KHR_wayland_surface. By abstracting the windowing system, your core rendering code can remain platform-independent while only the initialization code changes.

Setting Up Cross-Platform Vulkan Projects

WHEN DEVELOPING A MULTI-platform Vulkan application, the goal is to maintain a single codebase that can be compiled and executed on multiple platforms with minimal changes. Here are the essential steps and tools to set up a cross-platform project:

Choose a Build System: Use a cross-platform build system like **CMake**. CMake allows you to define build configurations that work on Windows, macOS, and Linux.

Example CMake Configuration:

cmake

cmake_minimum_required(VERSION 3.10)

project(VulkanApp)

```
set(CMAKE_CXX_STANDARD 17)

# Find Vulkan package

find_package(Vulkan REQUIRED)

# Include directories

include_directories(${Vulkan_INCLUDE_DIRS})

# Source files

set(SOURCES

src/main.cpp

src/vulkan_utils.cpp

src/vulkan_renderer.cpp

)

# Create executable

add_executable(VulkanApp ${SOURCES})

# Link Vulkan library

target_link_libraries(VulkanApp ${Vulkan_LIBRARIES})
```

1.

Platform-Specific Initialization: In your code, use preprocessor directives to handle platform-specific initialization. For instance, creating a Vulkan surface for different platforms can be managed with conditional compilation.

Example of Platform-Specific Surface Creation:

cpp

```
#ifdef _WIN32
VkWin32SurfaceCreateInfoKHR createInfo = {};
createInfo.sType = VK_STRUCTURE_TYPE_WIN32_SURFACE_CREATE_INFO_KH
createInfo.hwnd = hwnd; // Windows window handle
createInfo.hinstance = hInstance; // Windows instance handle
if (vkCreateWin32SurfaceKHR(instance, &createInfo, nullptr, &surface) != VK_SUCCESS) {
throw std::runtime_error("Failed to create Win32 surface!");
}
#elif defined(__linux__)
VkXcbSurfaceCreateInfoKHR createInfo = {};
createInfo.sType = VK_STRUCTURE_TYPE_XCB_SURFACE_CREATE_INFO_KHR;
createInfo.connection = connection; // XCB connection
createInfo.window = window; // XCB window
if (vkCreateXcbSurfaceKHR(instance, &createInfo, nullptr, &surface) != VK_SUCCESS) {
throw std::runtime_error("Failed to create XCB surface!");
}
#endif
```

2.

3. **Dependency Management**: Ensure that the Vulkan SDK and dependencies are correctly installed for each platform. For example:

○ **Windows**: Download and install the Vulkan SDK from LunarG.

○ **Linux**: Install via package managers (e.g., sudo apt install vulkan-sdk).

○ **macOS**: Use the Vulkan SDK with MoltenVK, a translation layer for Metal.

Managing Swapchains Across Platforms

SWAPCHAINS ARE CRITICAL for presenting images to the screen. Vulkan abstracts swapchains using surface extensions, which vary depending on the platform. Despite these variations, the core process of creating a swapchain remains the same.

Cross-Platform Swapchain Creation Code:

```
void createSwapchain() {

VkSwapchainCreateInfoKHR swapchainInfo = {};

swapchainInfo.sType =
VK_STRUCTURE_TYPE_SWAPCHAIN_CREATE_INFO_KHR;

swapchainInfo.surface = surface;

swapchainInfo.minImageCount = 2;

swapchainInfo.imageFormat = chosenFormat.format;
```

```
swapchainInfo.imageColorSpace = chosenFormat.colorSpace;

swapchainInfo.imageExtent = { width, height };

swapchainInfo.imageArrayLayers = 1;

swapchainInfo.imageUsage =
VK_IMAGE_USAGE_COLOR_ATTACHMENT_BIT;

swapchainInfo.imageSharingMode =
VK_SHARING_MODE_EXCLUSIVE;

swapchainInfo.preTransform =
VK_SURFACE_TRANSFORM_IDENTITY_BIT_KHR;

swapchainInfo.compositeAlpha =
VK_COMPOSITE_ALPHA_OPAQUE_BIT_KHR;

swapchainInfo.presentMode =
VK_PRESENT_MODE_FIFO_KHR;

swapchainInfo.clipped = VK_TRUE;

if (vkCreateSwapchainKHR(device, &swapchainInfo, nullptr,
&swapchain) != VK_SUCCESS) {

throw std::runtime_error("Failed to create swapchain!");

}

}
```

This code works across platforms as long as surface has been created using the appropriate platform-specific extension.

Handling Input and Window Management

FOR TRULY CROSS-PLATFORM applications, consider libraries such as **GLFW** or **SDL2** for input handling and window management. These libraries abstract platform-specific window creation and input events.

Using GLFW for Cross-Platform Window Creation:

```
if (!glfwInit()) {

throw std::runtime_error("Failed to initialize GLFW!");

}

glfwWindowHint(GLFW_CLIENT_API, GLFW_NO_API);

GLFWwindow* window = glfwCreateWindow(800, 600, "Vulkan Window", nullptr, nullptr);

if (!window) {

throw std::runtime_error("Failed to create GLFW window!");

}
```

GLFW automatically handles platform-specific details on Windows, macOS, and Linux, simplifying the process of creating a window and interfacing with Vulkan.

Best Practices for Cross-Platform Development

1. **Abstract Platform-Specific Code**: Encapsulate platform-specific code in separate functions or classes. This keeps your core logic clean and modular.
2. **Automated Testing**: Use CI/CD pipelines to build and test your application on multiple platforms (e.g., GitHub

Actions, GitLab CI, or Jenkins).

3. **Error Handling and Logging**: Implement robust error handling and logging to diagnose issues across platforms easily.
4. **Unified Shaders**: Write shaders in GLSL or HLSL and compile them to SPIR-V using tools like glslang or DXC to ensure compatibility across different platforms.
5. **Performance Optimization**: Profile your application on each platform, as performance bottlenecks can vary based on hardware and operating systems.

BY ADHERING TO THESE strategies, you can create efficient and maintainable Vulkan applications that provide consistent performance across a wide range of platforms.

Cross-Platform Rendering Pipelines

CREATING A CROSS-PLATFORM rendering pipeline in Vulkan is essential for ensuring that your graphics applications deliver consistent and optimal performance across various platforms, including Windows, Linux, macOS, and mobile devices. Unlike older APIs, Vulkan allows developers to create low-level, finely-tuned rendering pipelines that are customizable for different hardware and platforms.

This section explores the key aspects of building and managing Vulkan rendering pipelines that work seamlessly across platforms. We will cover pipeline creation, shader management, descriptor sets, and how to handle platform-specific optimizations.

Understanding Vulkan Rendering Pipelines

IN VULKAN, A RENDERING pipeline is a collection of state configurations and shader programs that dictate how rendering commands are processed and how graphics are drawn. Vulkan pipelines are highly configurable, and once created, they cannot be modified dynamically. This immutability is part of Vulkan's design for maximizing performance.

A typical Vulkan pipeline consists of the following stages:

1. **Vertex Input Stage**: Defines the format and structure of vertex data.
2. **Vertex Shader Stage**: Processes vertices and performs transformations.
3. **Tessellation Control and Evaluation Stages** (optional): Handle tessellation for complex geometries.
4. **Geometry Shader Stage** (optional): Generates or modifies primitives.
5. **Rasterization Stage**: Converts vertices into fragments (pixels).
6. **Fragment Shader Stage**: Processes fragments and determines their final color.
7. **Color Blending Stage**: Combines fragment output with existing frame buffer contents.
8. **Depth and Stencil Tests**: Manage depth and stencil operations.

Pipeline Creation Process

THE PROCESS OF CREATING a Vulkan pipeline involves multiple steps, each of which must be explicitly defined. Here's a breakdown of the essential steps:

1. **Shader Modules**: Load and compile SPIR-V shader modules.
2. **Fixed Function State**: Configure fixed function stages

(input assembly, rasterization, etc.).
3. **Descriptor Sets and Layouts**: Define how resources (uniforms, textures) are bound to shaders.
4. **Render Pass**: Specify how attachments (color, depth) are handled during rendering.
5. **Pipeline Layout**: Combine shader stages and fixed function states into a single layout.
6. **Pipeline Cache**: Optimize pipeline creation by reusing cached data.

Example of Basic Pipeline Creation

HERE'S AN EXAMPLE OF creating a basic Vulkan graphics pipeline:

```
VkPipeline createGraphicsPipeline(VkDevice device, VkRenderPass renderPass) {

// Load vertex and fragment shaders

VkShaderModule vertShaderModule = loadShaderModule("shaders/vert.spv", device);

VkShaderModule fragShaderModule = loadShaderModule("shaders/frag.spv", device);

// Vertex shader stage

VkPipelineShaderStageCreateInfo vertShaderStageInfo = {};

vertShaderStageInfo.sType = VK_STRUCTURE_TYPE_PIPELINE_SHADER_STAGE_CREATE_

vertShaderStageInfo.stage = VK_SHADER_STAGE_VERTEX_BIT;
```

```
vertShaderStageInfo.module = vertShaderModule;

vertShaderStageInfo.pName = "main";

// Fragment shader stage

VkPipelineShaderStageCreateInfo fragShaderStageInfo = {};

fragShaderStageInfo.sType =
VK_STRUCTURE_TYPE_PIPELINE_SHADER_STAGE_CREATE_

fragShaderStageInfo.stage =
VK_SHADER_STAGE_FRAGMENT_BIT;

fragShaderStageInfo.module = fragShaderModule;

fragShaderStageInfo.pName = "main";

VkPipelineShaderStageCreateInfo shaderStages[] = {
vertShaderStageInfo, fragShaderStageInfo };

// Input assembly

VkPipelineInputAssemblyStateCreateInfo inputAssembly = {};

inputAssembly.sType =
VK_STRUCTURE_TYPE_PIPELINE_INPUT_ASSEMBLY_STATE

inputAssembly.topology =
VK_PRIMITIVE_TOPOLOGY_TRIANGLE_LIST;

inputAssembly.primitiveRestartEnable = VK_FALSE;

// Viewport and scissor

VkViewport viewport = {};

viewport.x = 0.0f;
```

```
viewport.y = 0.0f;
viewport.width = (float)WIDTH;
viewport.height = (float)HEIGHT;
viewport.minDepth = 0.0f;
viewport.maxDepth = 1.0f;
VkRect2D scissor = {};
scissor.offset = {0, 0};
scissor.extent = {WIDTH, HEIGHT};
VkPipelineViewportStateCreateInfo viewportState = {};
viewportState.sType =
VK_STRUCTURE_TYPE_PIPELINE_VIEWPORT_STATE_CREATI
viewportState.viewportCount = 1;
viewportState.pViewports = &viewport;
viewportState.scissorCount = 1;
viewportState.pScissors = &scissor;
// Rasterizer
VkPipelineRasterizationStateCreateInfo rasterizer = {};
rasterizer.sType =
VK_STRUCTURE_TYPE_PIPELINE_RASTERIZATION_STATE_C
rasterizer.depthClampEnable = VK_FALSE;
rasterizer.rasterizerDiscardEnable = VK_FALSE;
```

```
rasterizer.polygonMode = VK_POLYGON_MODE_FILL;

rasterizer.lineWidth = 1.0f;

rasterizer.cullMode = VK_CULL_MODE_BACK_BIT;

rasterizer.frontFace = VK_FRONT_FACE_CLOCKWISE;

rasterizer.depthBiasEnable = VK_FALSE;

// Multisampling

VkPipelineMultisampleStateCreateInfo multisampling = {};

multisampling.sType =
VK_STRUCTURE_TYPE_PIPELINE_MULTISAMPLE_STATE_C

multisampling.sampleShadingEnable = VK_FALSE;

multisampling.rasterizationSamples =
VK_SAMPLE_COUNT_1_BIT;

// Color blending

VkPipelineColorBlendAttachmentState colorBlendAttachment =
{};

colorBlendAttachment.colorWriteMask =
VK_COLOR_COMPONENT_R_BIT |
VK_COLOR_COMPONENT_G_BIT |

VK_COLOR_COMPONENT_B_BIT |
VK_COLOR_COMPONENT_A_BIT;

colorBlendAttachment.blendEnable = VK_FALSE;

VkPipelineColorBlendStateCreateInfo colorBlending = {};
```

```
colorBlending.sType =
VK_STRUCTURE_TYPE_PIPELINE_COLOR_BLEND_STATE_CR

colorBlending.logicOpEnable = VK_FALSE;

colorBlending.attachmentCount = 1;

colorBlending.pAttachments = &colorBlendAttachment;

// Pipeline layout

VkPipelineLayoutCreateInfo pipelineLayoutInfo = {};

pipelineLayoutInfo.sType =
VK_STRUCTURE_TYPE_PIPELINE_LAYOUT_CREATE_INFO;

VkPipelineLayout pipelineLayout;

if (vkCreatePipelineLayout(device, &pipelineLayoutInfo, nullptr,
&pipelineLayout) != VK_SUCCESS) {

throw std::runtime_error("Failed to create pipeline layout!");

}

// Graphics pipeline

VkGraphicsPipelineCreateInfo pipelineInfo = {};

pipelineInfo.sType =
VK_STRUCTURE_TYPE_GRAPHICS_PIPELINE_CREATE_INFO;

pipelineInfo.stageCount = 2;

pipelineInfo.pStages = shaderStages;

pipelineInfo.pVertexInputState = &vertexInputInfo;

pipelineInfo.pInputAssemblyState = &inputAssembly;
```

```
pipelineInfo.pViewportState = &viewportState;
pipelineInfo.pRasterizationState = &rasterizer;
pipelineInfo.pMultisampleState = &multisampling;
pipelineInfo.pColorBlendState = &colorBlending;
pipelineInfo.layout = pipelineLayout;
pipelineInfo.renderPass = renderPass;
pipelineInfo.subpass = 0;
VkPipeline graphicsPipeline;
if (vkCreateGraphicsPipelines(device, VK_NULL_HANDLE, 1,
&pipelineInfo, nullptr, &graphicsPipeline) != VK_SUCCESS) {
throw std::runtime_error("Failed to create graphics pipeline!");
}
// Cleanup shaders after pipeline creation
vkDestroyShaderModule(device, vertShaderModule, nullptr);
vkDestroyShaderModule(device, fragShaderModule, nullptr);
return graphicsPipeline;
}
```

Portability Considerations for Pipelines

TO ENSURE YOUR PIPELINE works across platforms:

1. **Shader Compatibility**: Ensure shaders are compiled to SPIR-V, which is universally supported by Vulkan.

2. **Swapchain Formats**: Different platforms may have different surface formats and presentation modes. Query these formats and adapt your pipeline accordingly.
3. **Dynamic State**: Use dynamic states (e.g., viewport, scissor) where possible to minimize the number of pipeline objects you need to create.
4. **Pipeline Cache**: Use VkPipelineCache to store compiled pipelines for reuse across sessions, improving load times on all platforms.
5. **Validation Layers**: Enable validation layers during development to catch platform-specific issues early.

By following these practices, you can create efficient, portable, and maintainable Vulkan rendering pipelines suitable for a wide range of devices and platforms.

Best Practices for Multi-Device Support

IN MODERN GRAPHICS applications, ensuring robust support for multiple devices is critical for providing users with a seamless experience across diverse hardware configurations. Vulkan's low-level control and platform-agnostic design allow developers to effectively manage different GPUs, drivers, and system capabilities. However, handling multiple devices introduces challenges related to compatibility, performance optimization, and resource management.

This section explores strategies, techniques, and best practices for supporting multi-device environments in Vulkan. Topics covered include device selection, handling device capabilities, managing multiple GPUs, and optimizing performance for a wide range of hardware.

Device Selection and Initialization

VULKAN PROVIDES AN explicit mechanism for selecting and initializing devices through physical devices (VkPhysicalDevice). The process involves querying available GPUs, examining their properties, and selecting the most appropriate one based on application needs.

Enumerating Physical Devices

WHEN INITIALIZING VULKAN, the first step is to enumerate the available physical devices:

```
uint32_t deviceCount = 0;

vkEnumeratePhysicalDevices(instance, &deviceCount, nullptr);

if (deviceCount == 0) {

throw std::runtime_error("Failed to find GPUs with Vulkan support!");

}

std::vector<VkPhysicalDevice> devices(deviceCount);

vkEnumeratePhysicalDevices(instance, &deviceCount, devices.data());
```

Selecting the Best Physical Device

EACH PHYSICAL DEVICE has properties and features that can be queried to determine its suitability for your application. For example, you might prioritize a discrete GPU over an integrated GPU for performance reasons.

```
VkPhysicalDevice selectBestDevice(const std::vector<VkPhysicalDevice>& devices) {

for (const auto& device : devices) {

VkPhysicalDeviceProperties deviceProperties;

vkGetPhysicalDeviceProperties(device, &deviceProperties);

VkPhysicalDeviceFeatures deviceFeatures;

vkGetPhysicalDeviceFeatures(device, &deviceFeatures);

if (deviceProperties.deviceType == VK_PHYSICAL_DEVICE_TYPE_DISCRETE_GPU && deviceFeatures.geometryShader) {

return device;

}

}

throw std::runtime_error("Failed to find a suitable GPU!");

}
```

In this example, the function selects a discrete GPU that supports geometry shaders. You can expand the criteria based on the specific needs of your application, such as support for specific extensions, memory size, or queue families.

Querying Device Capabilities

DIFFERENT DEVICES MAY support varying levels of functionality, extensions, and limits. It is essential to query these capabilities and adapt your application accordingly.

Checking for Required Extensions

EXTENSIONS ENABLE ADDITIONAL functionality not included in the Vulkan core specification. Before creating a logical device, ensure that the required extensions are supported:

```
bool checkDeviceExtensionSupport(VkPhysicalDevice device, const std::vector<const char*>& requiredExtensions) {

uint32_t extensionCount;

vkEnumerateDeviceExtensionProperties(device, nullptr, &extensionCount, nullptr);

std::vector<VkExtensionProperties> availableExtensions(extensionCount);

vkEnumerateDeviceExtensionProperties(device, nullptr, &extensionCount, availableExtensions.data());

std::set<std::string> requiredExtensionSet(requiredExtensions.begin(), requiredExtensions.end());

for (const auto& extension : availableExtensions) {

requiredExtensionSet.erase(extension.extensionName);

}

return requiredExtensionSet.empty();

}
```

This function ensures that all required extensions are supported by the device before proceeding with initialization.

Handling Device Limits

VULKAN DEVICES HAVE hardware-specific limits that dictate maximum values for resources such as buffer sizes, image dimensions, and descriptor sets. Querying and respecting these limits is critical for avoiding crashes and undefined behavior.

```
VkPhysicalDeviceProperties properties;

vkGetPhysicalDeviceProperties(physicalDevice, &properties);

std::cout << "Max image dimension 2D: " << properties.limits.maxImageDimension2D << std::endl;

std::cout << "Max uniform buffer range: " << properties.limits.maxUniformBufferRange << std::endl;
```

If your application exceeds these limits, you may need to adjust resource usage dynamically based on the hardware capabilities.

Multi-GPU Support

IN SYSTEMS WITH MULTIPLE GPUs, Vulkan allows you to leverage additional hardware for rendering, compute operations, or other tasks. Multi-GPU support can enhance performance, provide redundancy, or enable advanced techniques such as frame splitting or parallel processing.

Types of Multi-GPU Configurations

1. **Explicit Multi-GPU (EMGPU)**: The application explicitly manages multiple GPUs, assigning tasks to each device. This approach offers maximum control but requires additional complexity in resource synchronization and management.

2. **Implicit Multi-GPU**: The system or driver automatically manages multiple GPUs, presenting them as a single logical device. This is simpler for developers but offers less control over hardware utilization.

Creating Multiple Logical Devices

TO UTILIZE MULTIPLE GPUs, you can create separate logical devices for each physical device:

```
std::vector<VkDevice> createMultipleLogicalDevices(const std::vector<VkPhysicalDevice>& physicalDevices) {

std::vector<VkDevice> logicalDevices;

for (const auto& physicalDevice : physicalDevices) {

VkDeviceCreateInfo createInfo = {};

createInfo.sType = VK_STRUCTURE_TYPE_DEVICE_CREATE_INFO;

createInfo.queueCreateInfoCount = 1;

createInfo.pQueueCreateInfos = &queueCreateInfo;

VkDevice device;

if (vkCreateDevice(physicalDevice, &createInfo, nullptr, &device) != VK_SUCCESS) {

throw std::runtime_error("Failed to create logical device!");

}

logicalDevices.push_back(device);
```

```
}
return logicalDevices;
}
```

Resource Synchronization Across Devices

WHEN USING MULTIPLE GPUs, managing resource synchronization is crucial to avoid race conditions and ensure data consistency. Techniques for synchronization include:

- **Semaphores**: Signal and wait operations to synchronize GPU workloads.
- **Fences**: CPU-GPU synchronization to ensure tasks complete before proceeding.
- **Memory Barriers**: Control access to resources shared between devices.

Example of Cross-GPU Synchronization with Semaphores:

```
VkSemaphoreCreateInfo semaphoreInfo = {};
semaphoreInfo.sType = VK_STRUCTURE_TYPE_SEMAPHORE_CREATE_INFO;
VkSemaphore semaphore;
if (vkCreateSemaphore(device, &semaphoreInfo, nullptr, &semaphore) != VK_SUCCESS) {
throw std::runtime_error("Failed to create semaphore!");
}
```

```
// Submit work to GPU1

VkSubmitInfo submitInfo = {};

submitInfo.sType =
VK_STRUCTURE_TYPE_SUBMIT_INFO;

submitInfo.signalSemaphoreCount = 1;

submitInfo.pSignalSemaphores = &semaphore;

vkQueueSubmit(queue1, 1, &submitInfo,
VK_NULL_HANDLE);

// Wait for GPU1 to finish before GPU2 starts

VkPipelineStageFlags waitStages[] = {
VK_PIPELINE_STAGE_COLOR_ATTACHMENT_OUTPUT_BIT
};

VkSubmitInfo waitSubmitInfo = {};

waitSubmitInfo.sType =
VK_STRUCTURE_TYPE_SUBMIT_INFO;

waitSubmitInfo.waitSemaphoreCount = 1;

waitSubmitInfo.pWaitSemaphores = &semaphore;

waitSubmitInfo.pWaitDstStageMask = waitStages;

vkQueueSubmit(queue2, 1, &waitSubmitInfo,
VK_NULL_HANDLE);
```

Performance Optimization for Multi-Device Support

SUPPORTING MULTIPLE devices requires careful performance optimization to ensure efficient resource usage across different hardware configurations.

1. **Adaptive Quality Settings**: Dynamically adjust graphical settings based on device capabilities. For example, reduce texture resolution or disable advanced effects on lower-end GPUs.
2. **Pipeline Caching**: Use pipeline caches to reduce the overhead of creating graphics pipelines, especially on devices with limited resources.
3. **Asynchronous Execution**: Leverage asynchronous compute or rendering to parallelize workloads and maximize hardware utilization.
4. **Profiling and Benchmarking**: Profile your application on different devices to identify bottlenecks and optimize accordingly. Tools like **RenderDoc**, **NVIDIA Nsight**, and **AMD Radeon GPU Profiler** are invaluable for this purpose.

Conclusion

SUPPORTING MULTIPLE devices in Vulkan requires a thorough understanding of device selection, capability querying, multi-GPU management, and performance optimization. By following these best practices, you can create robust, adaptable applications that deliver a consistent experience across a diverse range of hardware platforms.

Chapter 11: Case Studies and Real-World Applications

Game Development with Vulkan

VULKAN HAS QUICKLY become a powerful choice for modern game development due to its low-level control over hardware, efficient multi-threading, and explicit resource management. In this section, we'll explore how Vulkan fits into the game development pipeline, its advantages over older graphics APIs like OpenGL, and specific implementation strategies to leverage its capabilities. We'll also examine real-world examples of games and engines that use Vulkan, highlighting the performance benefits and challenges encountered along the way.

Why Vulkan for Game Development?

Performance and Efficiency

ONE OF THE BIGGEST draws of Vulkan is its performance-oriented design. By offering more direct control over GPU resources and avoiding unnecessary abstraction layers, developers can achieve higher frame rates and more consistent performance compared to legacy APIs.

In traditional APIs like OpenGL, a lot of state management and error-checking happens under the hood, which can create performance bottlenecks. Vulkan eliminates these implicit operations, allowing developers to optimize state changes, memory allocation, and resource management explicitly.

Multi-Threading Capabilities

MODERN CPUS COME WITH multiple cores, and utilizing these cores efficiently is crucial for performance in modern games. Vulkan is designed with multi-threading in mind, enabling concurrent creation of command buffers, parallel resource management, and asynchronous work submission to the GPU.

In contrast, APIs like OpenGL are largely single-threaded, meaning the majority of rendering tasks are limited to one thread. Vulkan's explicit multi-threading support allows developers to distribute rendering work across multiple threads, which can significantly reduce CPU bottlenecks.

Explicit Control Over Memory Management

MEMORY MANAGEMENT IS a critical aspect of modern game development, especially for high-fidelity games that require large textures, complex geometry, and extensive shader computations. Vulkan gives developers full control over memory allocation, allowing for more efficient use of GPU memory and minimizing fragmentation.

This level of control enables strategies like *memory pooling*, where multiple buffers and images are allocated from a single large block of memory to reduce overhead. It also allows developers to implement *custom allocators* to suit the needs of specific game engines.

Integrating Vulkan into Game Engines

Initial Setup and Abstractions

INTEGRATING VULKAN into a game engine requires significant effort due to its explicit nature. Most game engines create an abstraction layer over Vulkan to simplify the API for game developers. This abstraction layer handles tasks like:

1. **Initialization:** Setting up Vulkan instances, devices, queues, and swapchains.
2. **Resource Management:** Managing buffers, images, and memory allocations.
3. **Command Recording:** Simplifying command buffer creation and submission.
4. **Error Handling:** Abstracting Vulkan's verbose error-checking mechanisms.

An example of initializing Vulkan in a game engine might look like this:

```
VkApplicationInfo appInfo = {};

appInfo.sType = VK_STRUCTURE_TYPE_APPLICATION_INFO;

appInfo.pApplicationName = "My Vulkan Game";

appInfo.applicationVersion = VK_MAKE_VERSION(1, 0, 0);

appInfo.pEngineName = "My Game Engine";

appInfo.engineVersion = VK_MAKE_VERSION(1, 0, 0);

appInfo.apiVersion = VK_API_VERSION_1_2;
```

```
VkInstanceCreateInfo createInfo = {};

createInfo.sType                                          =
VK_STRUCTURE_TYPE_INSTANCE_CREATE_INFO;

createInfo.pApplicationInfo = &appInfo;

if (vkCreateInstance(&createInfo, nullptr, &instance) !=
VK_SUCCESS) {

throw std::runtime_error("Failed to create Vulkan instance!");

}
```

This snippet demonstrates the explicit nature of Vulkan's setup process, where each structure and parameter must be specified clearly.

Command Buffers and Rendering Loops

IN A VULKAN-BASED GAME engine, rendering work is encapsulated in *command buffers*. These buffers store commands to be executed by the GPU, such as drawing calls, state changes, and resource transitions.

A typical rendering loop in Vulkan looks like this:

1. **Acquire an Image from the Swapchain.**
2. **Record Commands into a Command Buffer.**
3. **Submit the Command Buffer to the Graphics Queue.**
4. **Present the Image to the Screen.**

Here's a simplified version of this loop:

```
// Acquire next image from the swapchain
```

```
vkAcquireNextImageKHR(device, swapchain, UINT64_MAX, imageAvailableSemaphore, VK_NULL_HANDLE, &imageIndex);

// Record commands

VkCommandBuffer commandBuffer = commandBuffers[imageIndex];

vkResetCommandBuffer(commandBuffer, 0);

recordCommandBuffer(commandBuffer, imageIndex);

// Submit the command buffer

VkSubmitInfo submitInfo = {};

submitInfo.sType = VK_STRUCTURE_TYPE_SUBMIT_INFO;

submitInfo.commandBufferCount = 1;

submitInfo.pCommandBuffers = &commandBuffer;

submitInfo.signalSemaphoreCount = 1;

submitInfo.pSignalSemaphores = &renderFinishedSemaphore;

vkQueueSubmit(graphicsQueue, 1, &submitInfo, inFlightFence);

// Present the image

VkPresentInfoKHR presentInfo = {};

presentInfo.sType = VK_STRUCTURE_TYPE_PRESENT_INFO_KHR;

presentInfo.swapchainCount = 1;
```

presentInfo.pSwapchains = &swapchain;

presentInfo.pImageIndices = &imageIndex;

vkQueuePresentKHR(presentQueue, &presentInfo);

This explicit control over command buffers allows developers to optimize rendering for specific game requirements.

Real-World Game Examples Using Vulkan

SEVERAL HIGH-PROFILE games and engines have adopted Vulkan to leverage its performance benefits. Some notable examples include:

Doom (2016) and Doom Eternal

DOOM (2016) was one of the first major titles to adopt Vulkan, developed by id Software using the id Tech 6 engine. By switching from OpenGL to Vulkan, the game saw significant performance improvements, particularly on lower-end hardware.

Key Benefits Achieved:

- **Higher Frame Rates:** Vulkan's low-level access allowed the game to achieve more consistent high frame rates.
- **Reduced CPU Bottlenecks:** Multi-threading capabilities enabled efficient use of multi-core CPUs.
- **Better Resource Management:** Explicit control over memory reduced resource overhead.

Wolfenstein II: The New Colossus

ANOTHER GAME DEVELOPED using the id Tech 6 engine, *Wolfenstein II* utilized Vulkan for its rendering pipeline. The game benefited from Vulkan's efficient handling of complex scenes and high-quality visual effects.

Dota 2

VALVE'S *Dota 2* was one of the first games to introduce Vulkan support. By offering Vulkan alongside DirectX, Valve demonstrated how Vulkan could achieve similar or better performance with reduced CPU usage.

Key Observations:

- **Lower Latency:** Vulkan reduced the time taken to process input and display frames.

- **Cross-Platform Support:** Vulkan's portability allowed for efficient support across Windows and Linux.

Challenges in Vulkan Game Development

WHILE VULKAN OFFERS numerous advantages, it also presents challenges that developers need to consider:

1. **Steep Learning Curve:** Vulkan's explicit nature means developers must manage many low-level details, which can be daunting compared to simpler APIs like OpenGL or DirectX 11.
2. **Complex Debugging:** Debugging Vulkan applications can be challenging due to the lack of implicit error handling. Tools like *Vulkan Validation Layers* are essential for

catching mistakes during development.

3. **Increased Development Time:** Writing and maintaining Vulkan code can take longer due to the need for detailed resource management and command setup.

Conclusion

VULKAN HAS PROVEN TO be a powerful tool for modern game development, offering low-level control, efficient multi-threading, and explicit memory management. While the learning curve is steep, the performance gains and flexibility it offers make it an attractive choice for developers aiming to push the boundaries of real-time rendering.

By integrating Vulkan into game engines, optimizing rendering loops, and learning from real-world case studies, developers can harness the full potential of this modern graphics API to create high-performance, visually stunning games.

Vulkan in Scientific Visualization

SCIENTIFIC VISUALIZATION is the process of graphically representing complex scientific data to aid in understanding, analysis, and communication. With the increasing complexity of datasets in fields like physics, chemistry, medicine, and climate science, visualization tools must efficiently handle large volumes of data while providing interactivity and clarity. Vulkan's low-level control, multi-threading support, and efficient handling of GPU resources make it an ideal API for scientific visualization applications.

This section explores how Vulkan is used in scientific visualization, its benefits, implementation strategies, and real-world use cases.

Why Vulkan for Scientific Visualization?

Handling Large Datasets

SCIENTIFIC DATASETS can be enormous, often containing millions or billions of data points. Vulkan's explicit memory management allows developers to allocate and manage GPU memory efficiently, reducing overhead and fragmentation. This capability is essential for visualizing large datasets without running into performance bottlenecks.

For example, in medical imaging, high-resolution MRI or CT scans can generate gigabytes of data. Vulkan's ability to control how this data is stored and accessed on the GPU ensures smooth visualization even when dealing with large textures and volume data.

Performance and Parallelism

SCIENTIFIC VISUALIZATION often involves computationally intensive tasks such as volume rendering, particle simulations, and fluid dynamics. Vulkan's support for multi-threaded command buffer creation and submission enables these tasks to be parallelized efficiently, leveraging multi-core CPUs and powerful GPUs.

Compute shaders in Vulkan can offload heavy computations to the GPU, such as processing large point clouds or performing complex mathematical transformations. This approach significantly speeds up visualization tasks compared to traditional CPU-based methods.

Cross-Platform Support

SCIENTIFIC RESEARCH often requires tools that work across different operating systems and hardware platforms. Vulkan's cross-platform nature ensures that visualization applications can run consistently on Windows, Linux, and macOS. This portability is particularly useful for research institutions and collaborative projects where diverse systems are used.

Key Concepts in Scientific Visualization with Vulkan

Volume Rendering

VOLUME RENDERING IS used to visualize three-dimensional scalar fields, such as medical scans, weather data, or fluid simulations. In Vulkan, volume rendering can be achieved using 3D textures and ray casting techniques.

A typical volume rendering pipeline involves the following steps:

1. **Load 3D Data:** Load the volume data into a 3D texture.
2. **Ray Casting:** Cast rays through the volume to sample data values and compute color and opacity.
3. **Transfer Function:** Apply a transfer function to map data values to colors and opacities.
4. **Rendering:** Accumulate sampled values and render the result to the screen.

Here's an example of setting up a 3D texture in Vulkan for volume rendering:

```
VkImageCreateInfo imageInfo = {};

imageInfo.sType = VK_STRUCTURE_TYPE_IMAGE_CREATE_INFO;

imageInfo.imageType = VK_IMAGE_TYPE_3D;

imageInfo.extent.width = volumeWidth;
```

```
imageInfo.extent.height = volumeHeight;

imageInfo.extent.depth = volumeDepth;

imageInfo.mipLevels = 1;

imageInfo.arrayLayers = 1;

imageInfo.format = VK_FORMAT_R8G8B8A8_UNORM;

imageInfo.tiling = VK_IMAGE_TILING_OPTIMAL;

imageInfo.initialLayout =
VK_IMAGE_LAYOUT_UNDEFINED;

imageInfo.usage =
VK_IMAGE_USAGE_TRANSFER_DST_BIT |
VK_IMAGE_USAGE_SAMPLED_BIT;

imageInfo.samples = VK_SAMPLE_COUNT_1_BIT;

imageInfo.sharingMode =
VK_SHARING_MODE_EXCLUSIVE;

VkImage volumeImage;

if (vkCreateImage(device, &imageInfo, nullptr, &volumeImage) !=
VK_SUCCESS) {

throw std::runtime_error("Failed to create 3D volume image!");

}
```

Point Cloud Visualization

POINT CLOUDS ARE COMMONLY used in fields like geology, archaeology, and robotics. They consist of large sets of points representing spatial data. Vulkan's ability to handle large buffers and parallel processing makes it well-suited for point cloud visualization.

To visualize a point cloud in Vulkan:

1. **Create a Vertex Buffer:** Store the positions, colors, and other attributes of the points in a vertex buffer.
2. **Shader Program:** Write a vertex and fragment shader to render the points.
3. **Render Loop:** Draw the points using the vkCmdDraw command.

Example of a simple vertex shader for rendering point clouds:

```
#version 450

layout(location = 0) in vec3 inPosition;

layout(location = 1) in vec3 inColor;

layout(location = 0) out vec3 fragColor;

layout(set = 0, binding = 0) uniform UBO {

mat4 modelViewProjection;

} ubo;

void main() {

gl_Position = ubo.modelViewProjection * vec4(inPosition, 1.0);

fragColor = inColor;

}
```

Compute Shaders for Data Processing

IN SCIENTIFIC VISUALIZATION, preprocessing data on the GPU can significantly improve performance. Compute shaders allow developers to perform tasks like filtering, transforming, or analyzing data in parallel.

Example of a compute shader for normalizing a dataset:

```
#version 450

layout(local_size_x = 256) in;

layout(set = 0, binding = 0) buffer DataBuffer {

float data[];

} bufferData;

void main() {

uint index = gl_GlobalInvocationID.x;

bufferData.data[index] = clamp(bufferData.data[index], 0.0, 1.0);

}
```

Real-World Applications of Vulkan in Scientific Visualization

Medical Imaging

IN MEDICAL IMAGING, tools like MRI and CT scanners generate large volumetric datasets that require efficient rendering and interaction. Vulkan enables applications to visualize these datasets in real-time, allowing doctors to explore scans interactively.

Example Use Cases:

- **3D Slicing:** View 2D slices of 3D data to examine specific layers.
- **Volume Ray Casting:** Render entire volumes with transparency to see internal structures.
- **Segmentation:** Highlight specific tissues or regions using compute shaders to process the data.

Climate and Weather Simulations

CLIMATE MODELS GENERATE massive datasets representing temperature, pressure, wind patterns, and more. Vulkan's efficient memory management and parallel processing capabilities allow scientists to visualize these datasets in high detail.

Example Use Cases:

- **Atmospheric Visualization:** Visualize global weather patterns and storm systems.
- **Fluid Dynamics:** Simulate and visualize ocean currents or air flow.
- **Heat Maps:** Represent temperature variations over large geographic regions.

Molecular Dynamics

IN CHEMISTRY AND BIOLOGY, visualizing molecular structures and interactions is essential for research and education.

Vulkan can handle the rendering of complex molecular models, including large proteins or DNA strands.

Example Use Cases:

- **Molecule Viewer:** Render large-scale molecular structures interactively.
- **Simulation Visualization:** Show real-time simulations of molecular interactions.
- **Binding Sites:** Visualize where molecules interact with enzymes or drugs.

Challenges in Vulkan-Based Scientific Visualization

Complexity of Implementation

VULKAN'S EXPLICIT CONTROL over resources and operations can make implementation challenging. Developers must carefully manage memory, synchronization, and pipeline configurations, which can increase development time.

Debugging and Validation

SCIENTIFIC VISUALIZATION applications often process large datasets, making it difficult to identify errors. Vulkan's verbose nature requires thorough use of validation layers and debugging tools to catch issues early.

Hardware Compatibility

WHILE VULKAN IS CROSS-platform, not all hardware supports the latest Vulkan features. Developers must ensure their applications work across different GPUs and operating systems, which may require fallback paths for older hardware.

Conclusion

VULKAN'S POWERFUL FEATURES make it an excellent choice for scientific visualization, offering the performance, flexibility, and cross-platform support needed to handle complex datasets. By leveraging volume rendering, point cloud visualization, and compute shaders, developers can create efficient and interactive tools for fields like medicine, climate science, and molecular dynamics.

Although the learning curve is steep, the benefits of using Vulkan for scientific visualization outweigh the challenges, enabling faster, more detailed, and more insightful representations of scientific data.

Industry Applications and Success Stories

VULKAN HAS PROVEN TO be a powerful tool across various industries, delivering performance improvements, efficient resource management, and cross-platform support. This section explores real-world industry applications where Vulkan has made a significant impact, examining how developers, companies, and software solutions have utilized Vulkan's capabilities to achieve their goals. These examples span game development, augmented reality (AR), virtual reality (VR), automotive technology, and scientific simulations.

Gaming Industry: Achieving High Performance and Scalability

Adoption by Major Game Engines

GAME ENGINES SERVE as the foundation for countless games, and integrating Vulkan into these engines offers developers significant performance improvements. Prominent engines have adopted Vulkan to provide a modern API alternative to legacy graphics APIs like OpenGL and DirectX.

- **Unreal Engine 4 and 5:** Epic Games' Unreal Engine supports Vulkan for high-performance rendering, particularly on mobile and VR platforms. By leveraging Vulkan, developers can achieve better frame rates and lower power consumption on mobile devices, essential for maintaining battery life while delivering high-quality visuals.

- **Unity:** Unity supports Vulkan on Android and desktop platforms, providing developers with more control over rendering and resource management. Vulkan's ability to reduce CPU bottlenecks allows mobile games to render more complex scenes without sacrificing performance.

Success Story: *Doom Eternal*

DOOM ETERNAL by id Software is a prime example of Vulkan's impact on gaming performance. The game utilizes the id Tech 7 engine, which fully supports Vulkan to achieve smooth, high-framerate gameplay even on lower-end hardware.

Key benefits of using Vulkan in *Doom Eternal*:

1. **Reduced CPU Overhead:** By using Vulkan's multi-threading capabilities, the game efficiently distributes rendering tasks across multiple CPU cores.
2. **Consistent Frame Rates:** Vulkan minimizes stuttering and frame drops, delivering a seamless experience.
3. **High-Quality Visual Effects:** Features like dynamic lighting, particle effects, and post-processing are optimized through Vulkan's efficient resource management.

Example of setting up a simple Vulkan render loop for a game engine:

```
void renderFrame() {

vkAcquireNextImageKHR(device, swapchain, UINT64_MAX, imageAvailableSemaphore, VK_NULL_HANDLE, &currentImageIndex);

VkSubmitInfo submitInfo = {};

submitInfo.sType = VK_STRUCTURE_TYPE_SUBMIT_INFO;

submitInfo.commandBufferCount = 1;

submitInfo.pCommandBuffers = &commandBuffers[currentImageIndex];

vkQueueSubmit(graphicsQueue, 1, &submitInfo, renderFence);

VkPresentInfoKHR presentInfo = {};

presentInfo.sType = VK_STRUCTURE_TYPE_PRESENT_INFO_KHR;

presentInfo.swapchainCount = 1;
```

```
presentInfo.pSwapchains = &swapchain;
presentInfo.pImageIndices = &currentImageIndex;
vkQueuePresentKHR(presentQueue, &presentInfo);
}
```

Virtual Reality (VR) and Augmented Reality (AR): Reducing Latency and Enhancing Immersion

Why Vulkan for VR and AR?

IN VR AND AR APPLICATIONS, minimizing latency and maintaining high frame rates are critical for delivering a smooth and immersive experience. Vulkan's low-level access and multi-threading capabilities allow developers to optimize rendering pipelines to meet these demanding requirements.

1. **Low Latency:** Vulkan reduces the time between input (head or hand movements) and visual feedback, minimizing motion sickness.
2. **Efficient Multi-Threading:** VR and AR applications benefit from Vulkan's ability to split rendering tasks across multiple threads, ensuring that complex scenes are processed efficiently.
3. **High Frame Rates:** Maintaining 90 frames per second (FPS) or higher is essential for VR comfort, and Vulkan's efficiency helps achieve this goal.

Success Story: Oculus and Vulkan

OCULUS HAS INTEGRATED Vulkan support into its development tools for the Oculus Quest and Quest 2 headsets. This integration allows developers to create high-performance VR experiences with optimized rendering and efficient use of hardware resources.

Key benefits:

- **Battery Efficiency:** Vulkan helps reduce power consumption, extending the battery life of standalone VR headsets.
- **Complex Scenes:** Developers can render detailed environments and dynamic lighting effects without compromising performance.
- **Cross-Platform Support:** Vulkan's support for Android and Windows enables seamless development for multiple VR platforms.

Automotive Industry: Advanced Infotainment and Simulation

Infotainment Systems

MODERN VEHICLES FEATURE sophisticated infotainment systems that deliver navigation, entertainment, and real-time vehicle data. Vulkan is increasingly being adopted to power these systems due to its efficiency and ability to render complex UIs smoothly.

- **3D Navigation Maps:** Vulkan's performance enables real-time rendering of 3D maps with dynamic elements like traffic data and terrain details.

- **Responsive Interfaces:** Infotainment systems can provide responsive touch interfaces with smooth animations and transitions.

Example of rendering a 3D map in an infotainment system using Vulkan:

```
void drawMapFrame() {

recordCommandBuffer(mapCommandBuffer);

VkSubmitInfo submitInfo = {};

submitInfo.sType =
VK_STRUCTURE_TYPE_SUBMIT_INFO;

submitInfo.commandBufferCount = 1;

submitInfo.pCommandBuffers = &mapCommandBuffer;

vkQueueSubmit(graphicsQueue, 1, &submitInfo,
mapRenderFence);

vkQueuePresentKHR(presentQueue, &presentInfo);

}
```

Simulation and Autonomous Driving

AUTONOMOUS VEHICLES rely on simulations to test driving algorithms and sensor data interpretation. Vulkan enables real-time simulation of traffic scenarios, environments, and sensor inputs.

- **Sensor Data Visualization:** Vulkan can render data from LIDAR, cameras, and radar in real-time, providing visual feedback for developers testing autonomous driving algorithms.

- **Scenario Simulation:** Vulkan-based engines can simulate complex driving environments to train AI models safely before real-world testing.

Scientific and Engineering Simulations

Fluid Dynamics and Physics Simulations

INDUSTRIES LIKE AEROSPACE, mechanical engineering, and environmental science use fluid dynamics simulations to model airflow, water currents, and other physical phenomena. Vulkan accelerates these simulations through compute shaders and efficient GPU utilization.

Example of a compute shader for fluid simulation:

```
#version 450

layout(local_size_x = 16, local_size_y = 16) in;

layout(set = 0, binding = 0) buffer FluidData {

vec4 velocity[];

} fluid;

void main() {

uint idx = gl_GlobalInvocationID.x + gl_GlobalInvocationID.y * 256;

fluid.velocity[idx] += vec4(0.0, -9.81, 0.0, 0.0) * 0.01; // Apply gravity
```

```
}
```

Molecular Dynamics

PHARMACEUTICAL COMPANIES and research institutions use molecular dynamics simulations to study protein folding, drug interactions, and chemical reactions. Vulkan's efficiency allows these simulations to run faster, providing quicker insights.

Key benefits:

- **Real-Time Visualization:** Researchers can visualize simulations as they run, aiding in analysis and hypothesis testing.
- **Large Data Sets:** Vulkan handles large molecular data sets with explicit memory management, ensuring smooth performance.

Media and Entertainment: Real-Time Video Processing

Video Editing and Effects

APPLICATIONS LIKE VIDEO editors and compositors benefit from Vulkan's low-level control for real-time video processing and effects rendering.

- **Color Grading:** Apply real-time color grading and corrections with compute shaders.
- **Video Effects:** Implement effects like motion blur, chroma keying, and transitions with efficient GPU processing.

Example of applying a compute shader for color correction:

```
#version 450

layout(local_size_x = 16, local_size_y = 16) in;

layout(set = 0, binding = 0) buffer ImageBuffer {

vec4 pixels[];

} image;

void main() {

uint idx = gl_GlobalInvocationID.x + gl_GlobalInvocationID.y *
imageWidth;

vec4 color = image.pixels[idx];

image.pixels[idx] = vec4(color.r * 1.1, color.g * 1.0, color.b * 0.9, 1.0);

}
```

Conclusion

VULKAN'S VERSATILITY and efficiency have made it an essential tool across numerous industries. From gaming and VR to automotive technology, scientific simulations, and media applications, Vulkan enables developers to achieve high performance, scalability, and cross-platform compatibility. The adoption of Vulkan continues to grow as more industries recognize its potential to solve complex rendering and computation challenges.

Chapter 12: Conclusion and Future of Vulkan

Recap of Key Concepts

IN THIS CHAPTER, WE revisit the core principles, ideas, and techniques that have been covered throughout the book. Vulkan is a powerful, low-overhead graphics API designed to give developers more control over the GPU while maximizing efficiency, performance, and flexibility. Mastery of Vulkan is not just about understanding individual concepts, but about seeing how they integrate into a coherent workflow for real-world applications. Let's reflect on what we've learned, breaking it down into key areas.

Graphics API Evolution

WE BEGAN BY UNDERSTANDING the historical context and evolution of graphics APIs. Vulkan represents a significant departure from older APIs like OpenGL due to its emphasis on explicit control, predictable performance, and parallelism. Unlike traditional APIs that abstract away many details, Vulkan exposes the underlying hardware more directly, giving developers the opportunity to optimize performance but also placing more responsibility in their hands.

Key points:

- **Immediate vs. Deferred Rendering**: Vulkan uses a deferred model where work is prepared ahead of time via command buffers and submitted to the GPU when ready.
- **Threading Model**: Unlike single-threaded APIs, Vulkan is designed to take advantage of multi-core CPUs

by enabling parallel command buffer generation and submission.

Vulkan Ecosystem

UNDERSTANDING THE VULKAN ecosystem is crucial. Vulkan is supported across multiple platforms, including Windows, Linux, Android, and macOS (via MoltenVK). The ecosystem includes tools like the Vulkan SDK, validation layers, and performance analysis tools that streamline the development and debugging processes.

Highlights of the Vulkan ecosystem:

1. **Vulkan SDK**: Provides essential libraries, headers, and tools for developing Vulkan applications.
2. **Validation Layers**: Debugging aids that ensure proper API usage.
3. **SPIR-V**: The intermediate shader language for Vulkan, which decouples high-level shading languages like GLSL from the API itself.
4. **Tools**: Graphics debuggers like RenderDoc, API tracers, and profilers help identify bottlenecks and optimize performance.

Core Concepts and Architecture

AT THE HEART OF VULKAN is its architecture, which is built around explicit control and flexibility. Some of the core concepts are:

- **Command Buffers**: Pre-recorded sequences of commands that the GPU can execute. These are submitted to **Queues**, which handle the actual processing.

- **Pipelines**: Descriptions of the rendering process that combine shaders, states, and configurations.

- **Memory Management**: Unlike older APIs, Vulkan requires the developer to explicitly manage GPU memory allocation.

Understanding these fundamentals is essential to harnessing the full power of Vulkan.

Example: Creating a Simple Command Buffer

```
VKCOMMANDBUFFERALLOCATEINFO allocInfo{};

allocInfo.sType =
VK_STRUCTURE_TYPE_COMMAND_BUFFER_ALLOCATE_I

allocInfo.commandPool = commandPool;

allocInfo.level =
VK_COMMAND_BUFFER_LEVEL_PRIMARY;

allocInfo.commandBufferCount = 1;

VkCommandBuffer commandBuffer;

vkAllocateCommandBuffers(device, &allocInfo,
&commandBuffer);

// Start recording

VkCommandBufferBeginInfo beginInfo{};
```

```
beginInfo.sType =
VK_STRUCTURE_TYPE_COMMAND_BUFFER_BEGIN_INFO;

vkBeginCommandBuffer(commandBuffer, &beginInfo);

// Record commands

vkCmdBindPipeline(commandBuffer,
VK_PIPELINE_BIND_POINT_GRAPHICS, graphicsPipeline);

vkCmdDraw(commandBuffer, 3, 1, 0, 0);

// End recording

vkEndCommandBuffer(commandBuffer);
```

This code snippet demonstrates how Vulkan requires detailed setup and control over command buffer allocation, recording, and execution.

Pipeline Management

PIPELINES ARE ONE OF the most complex yet essential aspects of Vulkan. Unlike dynamic state-based APIs, Vulkan pipelines are created ahead of time and cannot be modified once they are compiled. This design allows for greater performance optimization but requires careful planning.

Key pipeline stages include:

- **Input Assembly**: Handles vertex data input.
- **Rasterization**: Converts primitives into fragments.
- **Fragment Shader**: Determines the color of each fragment.

- **Output Merger**: Combines fragments and writes them to the framebuffer.

Pipelines in Vulkan are immutable, so managing multiple pipelines or creating pipeline variants for different configurations becomes an important consideration in any Vulkan application.

Example: Pipeline Creation Overview

VKPIPELINESHADERSTAGECREATEINFO vertShaderStageInfo{};

vertShaderStageInfo.sType = VK_STRUCTURE_TYPE_PIPELINE_SHADER_STAGE_CREATE_

vertShaderStageInfo.stage = VK_SHADER_STAGE_VERTEX_BIT;

vertShaderStageInfo.module = vertShaderModule;

vertShaderStageInfo.pName = "main";

VkPipelineShaderStageCreateInfo fragShaderStageInfo{};

fragShaderStageInfo.sType = VK_STRUCTURE_TYPE_PIPELINE_SHADER_STAGE_CREATE_

fragShaderStageInfo.stage = VK_SHADER_STAGE_FRAGMENT_BIT;

fragShaderStageInfo.module = fragShaderModule;

fragShaderStageInfo.pName = "main";

VkPipelineShaderStageCreateInfo shaderStages[] = {vertShaderStageInfo, fragShaderStageInfo};

In the snippet above, we prepare two shader stages – vertex and fragment – for a graphics pipeline.

Memory Management

MEMORY MANAGEMENT IN Vulkan is explicit and critical for optimal performance. Vulkan offers flexibility but requires careful planning for resource allocation and synchronization. Developers must allocate memory manually and manage it through buffers, images, and descriptors.

Key Takeaways:

1. **Memory Heaps and Types**: Vulkan exposes different memory types that correspond to GPU and CPU capabilities.
2. **Buffers and Images**: Used for storing vertex data, textures, and more.
3. **Synchronization**: Ensures proper sequencing of GPU tasks using fences, semaphores, and barriers.

Example: Allocating Buffer Memory

```
VKMEMORYREQUIREMENTS memRequirements;

vkGetBufferMemoryRequirements(device, buffer, &memRequirements);

VkMemoryAllocateInfo allocInfo{};

allocInfo.sType = VK_STRUCTURE_TYPE_MEMORY_ALLOCATE_INFO;

allocInfo.allocationSize = memRequirements.size;
```

```
allocInfo.memoryTypeIndex =
findMemoryType(memRequirements.memoryTypeBits,
VK_MEMORY_PROPERTY_HOST_VISIBLE_BIT |
VK_MEMORY_PROPERTY_HOST_COHERENT_BIT);

VkDeviceMemory bufferMemory;

vkAllocateMemory(device, &allocInfo, nullptr, &bufferMemory);

vkBindBufferMemory(device, buffer, bufferMemory, 0);
```

Synchronization and Rendering Workflow

SYNCHRONIZATION PRIMITIVES such as semaphores, fences, and barriers ensure smooth execution and prevent race conditions.

- **Semaphores**: Used to synchronize operations between the GPU's different stages.
- **Fences**: Used to synchronize the CPU with GPU work.
- **Barriers**: Ensure data visibility and proper execution order when transitioning resource states.

Efficient synchronization is essential for high-performance Vulkan applications.

Debugging and Optimization

DEBUGGING AND OPTIMIZING Vulkan applications can be challenging due to the API's complexity. Vulkan provides powerful tools such as:

- **Validation Layers**: Catch API misuse and provide detailed error messages.
- **Profilers**: Identify performance bottlenecks.
- **API Tracers**: Record API calls for detailed inspection.

Example: Enabling Validation Layers

```
VKDEBUGUTILSMESSENGERCREATEINFOEXT
createInfo{};

createInfo.sType =
VK_STRUCTURE_TYPE_DEBUG_UTILS_MESSENGER_CREATE

createInfo.messageSeverity =
VK_DEBUG_UTILS_MESSAGE_SEVERITY_VERBOSE_BIT_EXT
|
VK_DEBUG_UTILS_MESSAGE_SEVERITY_WARNING_BIT_EXT
|
VK_DEBUG_UTILS_MESSAGE_SEVERITY_ERROR_BIT_EXT;

createInfo.messageType =
VK_DEBUG_UTILS_MESSAGE_TYPE_GENERAL_BIT_EXT
|
VK_DEBUG_UTILS_MESSAGE_TYPE_VALIDATION_BIT_EXT
|
VK_DEBUG_UTILS_MESSAGE_TYPE_PERFORMANCE_BIT_EX

createInfo.pfnUserCallback = debugCallback;
```

Conclusion

MASTERING VULKAN REQUIRES practice, experimentation, and patience. Each concept — from command buffers to pipelines, from memory management to debugging — contributes to the overall power and flexibility of Vulkan. By revisiting these key ideas, you can develop high-performance, cross-platform graphics and compute applications.

This recap sets the foundation for continuing your journey with Vulkan. Whether you're developing games, simulations, or other graphics-intensive applications, the knowledge gained here will serve as a robust starting point.

Emerging Trends in Graphics APIs

THE WORLD OF GRAPHICS APIs is rapidly evolving, shaped by both hardware advancements and the growing demands of real-time applications. Vulkan has solidified its position as a cutting-edge, low-overhead API, but the future holds exciting new developments that will continue to shape graphics programming. In this section, we will explore some of the most prominent trends influencing the future of graphics APIs. These include ray tracing, dynamic rendering, machine learning integration, virtual reality, multi-threaded rendering, and more. Each trend highlights how graphics APIs are adapting to meet the needs of modern and next-generation applications.

Ray Tracing and Real-Time Rendering

RAY TRACING HAS LONG been used in pre-rendered graphics due to its ability to produce photorealistic lighting, shadows, and reflections. With the advent of modern GPUs and the introduction of ray tracing extensions in Vulkan, real-time ray tracing is now feasible for games and interactive applications.

Vulkan Ray Tracing

VULKAN SUPPORTS RAY tracing through the VK_KHR_ray_tracing_pipeline extension, allowing developers to implement sophisticated lighting effects that were previously impractical in real-time. Ray tracing in Vulkan involves several key components:

1. **Acceleration Structures**: Data structures that enable efficient ray intersection tests.
2. **Ray Tracing Pipelines**: Similar to graphics pipelines but designed for tracing rays.
3. **Shader Binding Tables (SBT)**: Define the relationship between rays and shaders.

Example: Setting Up Ray Tracing Pipeline

```
VKRAYTRACINGPIPELINECREATEINFOKHR
rayTracingPipelineCI{};

rayTracingPipelineCI.sType =
VK_STRUCTURE_TYPE_RAY_TRACING_PIPELINE_CREATE_I

rayTracingPipelineCI.stageCount = shaderStages.size();

rayTracingPipelineCI.pStages = shaderStages.data();

rayTracingPipelineCI.groupCount = shaderGroups.size();

rayTracingPipelineCI.pGroups = shaderGroups.data();

rayTracingPipelineCI.maxPipelineRayRecursionDepth = 1;

VkPipeline rayTracingPipeline;
```

vkCreateRayTracingPipelinesKHR(device, VK_NULL_HANDLE, 1, &rayTracingPipelineCI, nullptr, &rayTracingPipeline);

Future of Ray Tracing

AS HARDWARE CONTINUES to improve, real-time ray tracing will become more accessible and less performance-intensive. Hybrid rendering techniques that combine traditional rasterization with ray tracing are likely to dominate in the coming years, offering a balance between performance and visual quality.

Dynamic Rendering

STATIC RENDER PASSES and framebuffers have been a staple in Vulkan, but dynamic rendering introduces greater flexibility. The VK_KHR_dynamic_rendering extension allows developers to specify rendering information at command recording time, rather than upfront during pipeline creation.

Benefits of Dynamic Rendering

1. **Simplified API**: Reduces the need for multiple render pass objects.
2. **Flexibility**: Supports dynamic framebuffer attachments and formats.
3. **Performance**: Avoids the overhead of creating and managing multiple render passes.

Example: Using Dynamic Rendering

VKRENDERINGATTACHMENTINFO colorAttachment{};

```
colorAttachment.sType = VK_STRUCTURE_TYPE_RENDERING_ATTACHMENT_INFO;
colorAttachment.imageView = swapchainImageViews[i];
colorAttachment.imageLayout = VK_IMAGE_LAYOUT_COLOR_ATTACHMENT_OPTIMAL;
colorAttachment.loadOp = VK_ATTACHMENT_LOAD_OP_CLEAR;
colorAttachment.storeOp = VK_ATTACHMENT_STORE_OP_STORE;
colorAttachment.clearValue.color = {0.0f, 0.0f, 0.0f, 1.0f};
VkRenderingInfo renderingInfo{};
renderingInfo.sType = VK_STRUCTURE_TYPE_RENDERING_INFO;
renderingInfo.renderArea = {{0, 0}, swapchainExtent};
renderingInfo.layerCount = 1;
renderingInfo.colorAttachmentCount = 1;
renderingInfo.pColorAttachments = &colorAttachment;
vkCmdBeginRendering(commandBuffer, &renderingInfo);
vkCmdDraw(commandBuffer, 3, 1, 0, 0);
vkCmdEndRendering(commandBuffer);
```

Dynamic rendering simplifies rendering workflows and is expected to play a significant role in future Vulkan applications.

Machine Learning Integration

THE INTEGRATION OF machine learning (ML) into graphics workflows is transforming rendering techniques. AI-based solutions like **DLSS (Deep Learning Super Sampling)** and **AI-driven denoising** are becoming more prevalent, offering performance gains and improved image quality.

Applications of Machine Learning in Graphics

1. **Super Resolution**: Techniques like DLSS upscale lower-resolution images to higher resolutions while maintaining visual fidelity.
2. **Denoising**: AI-based denoisers reduce noise in ray-traced images, speeding up rendering times.
3. **Animation and Physics**: ML-driven approaches generate realistic animations and simulate complex physics.

Vulkan and ML

WHILE VULKAN DOES NOT natively provide machine learning operations, compute shaders can be used to implement custom ML models. Additionally, APIs like OpenCL, CUDA, and libraries like TensorRT can be integrated with Vulkan applications for AI-powered rendering.

Virtual Reality (VR) and Augmented Reality (AR)

THE DEMAND FOR IMMERSIVE experiences in VR and AR is driving innovations in graphics APIs. Vulkan's low-level control and efficiency make it an ideal choice for VR applications, where high frame rates and low latency are critical.

Challenges in VR

1. **Latency**: Minimizing the delay between user actions and visual updates is essential.
2. **Performance**: Maintaining a consistent frame rate of 90 FPS or higher is required for a smooth experience.
3. **Stereoscopic Rendering**: Rendering scenes from two different viewpoints for each eye.

Vulkan Features for VR

- **Multi-View Rendering**: The VK_KHR_multiview extension allows efficient rendering of multiple views in a single pass.

- **Asynchronous Timewarp**: Reduces perceived latency by adjusting the final rendered image based on head movement.

Example: Multi-View Setup

```
VKRENDERPASSMULTIVIEWCREATEINFO
multiviewInfo{};

multiviewInfo.sType =
VK_STRUCTURE_TYPE_RENDER_PASS_MULTIVIEW_CREATE_

multiviewInfo.subpassCount = 1;

multiviewInfo.pViewMasks = &viewMask;
```

Vulkan's continued development will likely include more features tailored to VR and AR.

Multi-Threaded Rendering

AS CPUS BECOME MORE powerful with increasing core counts, multi-threaded rendering is essential for fully utilizing available hardware. Vulkan's design encourages multi-threading, allowing developers to record command buffers in parallel and submit them to different queues.

Key Techniques

1. **Threaded Command Buffer Generation**: Each thread records command buffers independently.
2. **Parallel Resource Loading**: Load textures, buffers, and shaders concurrently.
3. **Synchronization Management**: Ensure proper synchronization between threads using fences and semaphores.

Example: Multi-Threaded Command Buffer Recording

```
STD::VECTOR<STD::THREAD> threads;

for (int i = 0; i < threadCount; i++) {

threads.emplace_back([&, i]() {

VkCommandBuffer cmdBuffer = allocateCommandBuffer();

vkBeginCommandBuffer(cmdBuffer, &beginInfo);

// Record commands...

vkEndCommandBuffer(cmdBuffer);

});
```

```
}
for (auto& thread : threads) {
thread.join();
}
```

Effective multi-threading can significantly boost performance in complex applications.

Portability and Cross-Platform Development

WITH VULKAN'S SUPPORT for multiple platforms, developing portable applications is more achievable than ever. Tools like **MoltenVK** allow Vulkan applications to run on Apple's platforms by translating Vulkan calls to Metal.

Best Practices for Portability

1. **Abstraction Layers**: Create platform-independent abstractions for windowing, input, and rendering.
2. **Feature Querying**: Check for supported features and extensions at runtime.
3. **Cross-Platform Shaders**: Use SPIR-V to compile shaders once and deploy them across platforms.

Conclusion

THE FUTURE OF GRAPHICS APIs is shaped by innovations in real-time ray tracing, dynamic rendering, AI integration, virtual reality, and multi-threading. Vulkan's design makes it well-suited to adapt to these emerging trends, offering developers the tools needed to create high-performance, next-generation applications. As technology continues to evolve, staying informed about these trends and incorporating them into your workflow will be key to mastering graphics development.

Continuing Your Vulkan Journey

VULKAN IS A POWERFUL, low-level API designed for developers who want complete control over GPU operations and rendering workflows. While this book covers the fundamentals, mastering Vulkan requires continuous learning, hands-on experience, and keeping up with industry developments. In this section, we'll outline various pathways, resources, practices, and projects to help you grow your Vulkan skills and integrate them into real-world applications.

---

1. Building Projects and Demos

THE BEST WAY TO SOLIDIFY your Vulkan knowledge is to work on practical projects. Start with small demos, gradually increasing complexity as you become more comfortable with the API.

Project Ideas:

1. **Basic 3D Renderer**: Build a simple application that renders a rotating 3D model with basic lighting and shading.
2. **Deferred Shading Engine**: Implement a deferred rendering pipeline, which separates geometry rendering from lighting calculations to handle complex scenes efficiently.
3. **Particle System**: Develop a particle system using compute shaders to simulate fire, smoke, or water effects.

4. **Ray Tracing Demo**: Create a basic real-time ray tracing demo using Vulkan's ray tracing extensions. Start with simple reflections and shadows, then add complexity.
5. **Post-Processing Effects**: Implement visual effects like bloom, motion blur, and screen-space ambient occlusion (SSAO) to learn about full-screen passes and image processing.
6. **Game Engine Prototype**: Develop a minimalistic game engine that supports model loading, input handling, and basic physics.

Example: Creating a Basic 3D Renderer

```
// LOAD AND COMPILE VERTEX and fragment shaders

VkShaderModule vertexShader = createShaderModule("shaders/vertex.spv");

VkShaderModule fragmentShader = createShaderModule("shaders/fragment.spv");

// Create a graphics pipeline

VkPipelineShaderStageCreateInfo vertShaderStageInfo = {};

vertShaderStageInfo.sType = VK_STRUCTURE_TYPE_PIPELINE_SHADER_STAGE_CREATE_I

vertShaderStageInfo.stage = VK_SHADER_STAGE_VERTEX_BIT;

vertShaderStageInfo.module = vertexShader;

vertShaderStageInfo.pName = "main";

VkPipelineShaderStageCreateInfo fragShaderStageInfo = {};
```

```
fragShaderStageInfo.sType =
VK_STRUCTURE_TYPE_PIPELINE_SHADER_STAGE_CREATE_

fragShaderStageInfo.stage =
VK_SHADER_STAGE_FRAGMENT_BIT;

fragShaderStageInfo.module = fragmentShader;

fragShaderStageInfo.pName = "main";

// Record command buffer

vkCmdBeginRenderPass(commandBuffer, &renderPassInfo,
VK_SUBPASS_CONTENTS_INLINE);

vkCmdBindPipeline(commandBuffer,
VK_PIPELINE_BIND_POINT_GRAPHICS, graphicsPipeline);

vkCmdDraw(commandBuffer, vertexCount, 1, 0, 0);

vkCmdEndRenderPass(commandBuffer);
```

Building these projects will help reinforce concepts like pipeline creation, memory management, and synchronization.

2. Contributing to Open-Source Projects

PARTICIPATING IN OPEN-source projects can accelerate your learning and connect you with the Vulkan development community.

Popular Vulkan Open-Source Projects:

1. **Vulkan Samples**: TheKhronosGroup Vulkan-Samples[3] repository contains comprehensive examples demonstrating various Vulkan features.

3. https://github.com/KhronosGroup/Vulkan-Samples

2. **RenderDoc**: A widely-used graphics debugger for Vulkan. Contributing to RenderDoc will give you insight into graphics debugging techniques.
3. **VulkanTools**: Tools and utilities provided by the Vulkan SDK. You can help improve validation layers, debugging tools, or performance analyzers.
4. **Games and Engines**: Open-source engines like **Godot Engine**, **Xenko**, or **Doom 3 (BFG Edition)** often have Vulkan render backends. Contributing to these engines will deepen your understanding of integrating Vulkan into large projects.

Steps to Contribute:

1. **Find an Issue**: Look for beginner-friendly issues labeled **"good first issue"** or **"help wanted"**.
2. **Fork the Repository**: Create a fork of the project on GitHub.
3. **Clone and Build**: Set up the project locally and ensure you can build it.
4. **Submit Pull Requests**: Once you've made changes, submit a pull request for review.

---

3. Staying Updated with Industry Trends

VULKAN IS CONTINUOUSLY evolving, with new extensions, features, and best practices being introduced. Staying informed is essential to ensure your skills remain relevant.

Key Resources for Updates:

1. **Khronos Group Website**: The official source for Vulkan news, specifications, and updates.

○ **Website**: https://www.khronos.org/vulkan

2. **Blogs and Articles**:

○ **NVIDIA Developer Blog**: Covers GPU-related developments and Vulkan optimizations.

○ **AMD GPUOpen**: Provides resources and tools for Vulkan development.

3. **YouTube Channels**:

○ **Khronos Group Channel**: Regularly posts Vulkan tutorials, updates, and conference talks.

○ **NVIDIA Developer**: Offers deep dives into graphics techniques and optimizations.

4. **Conferences and Events**:

○ **SIGGRAPH**: An annual conference showcasing cutting-edge graphics research.

○ **GDC (Game Developers Conference)**: Features Vulkan sessions, workshops, and panels.

4. Advanced Learning Resources

ONCE YOU HAVE A SOLID foundation, deepen your knowledge with advanced learning materials.

Books and Documentation:

1. **"Vulkan Programming Guide"** by Graham Sellers and John Kessenich: A detailed guide covering Vulkan fundamentals and best practices.
2. **Official Vulkan Specification**: The most authoritative resource on Vulkan, containing detailed explanations of every API function and structure.
3. **"GPU Zen" Series**: Collections of advanced GPU programming techniques, including Vulkan-based rendering methods.

Online Tutorials:

1. **LearnVulkan**: Step-by-step tutorials covering basic and advanced topics.
2. **Vulkan-Tutorial.com**: A comprehensive, beginner-friendly guide to Vulkan development.

---

5. Experimenting with Extensions

VULKAN'S MODULAR DESIGN allows for extensions that provide additional functionality. Learning to use these extensions can give you a competitive edge.

Notable Extensions:

1. **VK_KHR_ray_tracing_pipeline**: Enables real-time ray tracing.
2. **VK_KHR_dynamic_rendering**: Simplifies render pass creation.
3. **VK_EXT_descriptor_indexing**: Supports flexible descriptor indexing for modern rendering techniques.
4. **VK_KHR_multiview**: Facilitates efficient VR and stereo rendering.

Example: Using a Ray Tracing Extension

```
VKPHYSICALDEVICERAYTRACINGPIPELINEFEATURESKHR rtFeatures{};

rtFeatures.sType = VK_STRUCTURE_TYPE_PHYSICAL_DEVICE_RAY_TRACING_

rtFeatures.rayTracingPipeline = VK_TRUE;

// Include in the device creation info

VkDeviceCreateInfo createInfo{};

createInfo.sType = VK_STRUCTURE_TYPE_DEVICE_CREATE_INFO;

createInfo.pNext = &rtFeatures;
```

Experimenting with extensions allows you to stay at the forefront of graphics technology.

6. Engaging with the Community

BEING PART OF THE VULKAN community can enhance your learning and open up new opportunities.

Community Platforms:

1. **Reddit**: Subreddits liker/vulkan[4] andr/GraphicsProgramming[5] are great for discussions and advice.

2. **Discord Servers**:

○ **Khronos Group Discord**: Connect with Vulkan developers and Khronos members.

○ **Graphics Programming Discord**: A hub for graphics enthusiasts.

3. **Stack Overflow**: TheVulkan tag[6] is useful for finding solutions to specific issues.

4. **GitHub Discussions**: Many Vulkan projects host discussions on GitHub where you can ask questions or share knowledge.

Conclusion

CONTINUING YOUR VULKAN journey involves hands-on projects, open-source contributions, staying updated, experimenting

4. https://www.reddit.com/r/vulkan

5. https://www.reddit.com/r/GraphicsProgramming

6. https://stackoverflow.com/questions/tagged/vulkan

with extensions, and engaging with the community. The path to mastery requires dedication, but with Vulkan's growing relevance in graphics and compute applications, your efforts will be rewarded with deep insights and new opportunities in the world of graphics programming.

Chapter 13: Appendices

Glossary of Terms

IN THIS SECTION, WE provide a comprehensive glossary of terms relevant to Vulkan development. These definitions will serve as a quick reference for understanding key concepts, terminologies, and technologies associated with Vulkan and graphics programming. The glossary covers everything from fundamental principles to more advanced topics. Let's dive into the essential terms you need to be familiar with when working with Vulkan.

A

- **API (Application Programming Interface):** A set of functions and protocols that allow different software components to communicate. Vulkan is a modern graphics API that provides low-level access to GPU hardware.

- **Attachment:** A memory location that a render pass uses for reading or writing data. Examples include color attachments, depth attachments, and stencil attachments.

- **AS (Acceleration Structure):** A data structure used in ray tracing to efficiently intersect rays with scene geometry. Vulkan's ray tracing extensions make use of acceleration structures.

B

- **Barrier:** A synchronization primitive in Vulkan that ensures proper memory access and execution order. Examples include image memory barriers and buffer memory barriers.

- **Bind Point:** A specific point in the graphics or compute pipeline where resources, such as descriptor sets or shaders, are bound.

- **Buffer:** A region of memory used for storing data like vertices, indices, or uniform data. Buffers can be bound to different stages of the pipeline.

- **Buffer View:** A way to describe how to interpret a buffer's data, such as defining it as an array of a certain data type.

C

- **Command Buffer:** A container for recording GPU commands. Command buffers are submitted to a queue for execution.

- **Command Pool:** A pool from which command buffers are allocated. It manages the memory for command buffers.

- **Compute Pipeline:** A pipeline used for executing compute shaders. Unlike graphics pipelines, compute pipelines do not deal with rendering.

- **Culling:** The process of discarding primitives that are not visible to the camera, such as back-face culling or frustum culling.

D

- **Descriptor:** A structure that provides information about how to access resources like buffers or images in shaders.

- **Descriptor Pool:** A pool that manages the memory for descriptors. Descriptors are allocated from this pool.

- **Descriptor Set:** A collection of descriptors that are bound to a pipeline to provide resources to shaders.

- **Device:** Represents a logical GPU in Vulkan. Applications issue commands to a device to perform operations on the GPU.

- **Dynamic State:** Pipeline state that can be changed without creating a new pipeline object. Examples include viewport size and blend constants.

F

- **Fence:** A synchronization primitive used to determine when the GPU has completed certain tasks. Fences are often used to synchronize CPU and GPU work.

- **Framebuffer:** A collection of image views used as attachments during a render pass. It defines the output surfaces for rendering.

- **Fragment Shader:** A shader stage that processes fragments generated by rasterization. It computes the final color of each fragment.

- **Front-Face:** The face of a triangle that is considered to be the front based on the winding order of its vertices (clockwise or counter-clockwise).

G

- **Graphics Pipeline:** A series of stages (vertex shader, fragment shader, etc.) that process data to produce rendered images. The graphics pipeline defines how rendering is performed.

- **GPU (Graphics Processing Unit):** A specialized processor designed to accelerate graphics rendering and compute tasks.

- **Grid:** A collection of workgroups in compute shader execution. Each workgroup contains a set of threads (invocations).

I

- **Image:** A resource representing a 2D or 3D texture. Images are used as color attachments, depth attachments, or shader resources.

- **Image Layout:** The layout of an image in memory, such as VK_IMAGE_LAYOUT_COLOR_ATTACHMENT_OPTIMAL or VK_IMAGE_LAYOUT_SHADER_READ_ONLY_OPTIMAL.

- **Instance:** The top-level Vulkan object that initializes the API and provides access to physical devices.

- **Invocation:** A single execution of a shader program. For example, each fragment processed by a fragment shader is a separate invocation.

L

- **Layer:** Additional code that can be loaded into the Vulkan runtime to provide validation, debugging, or profiling capabilities. The **Validation Layers** are commonly used during development.

- **LOD (Level of Detail):** A technique for rendering objects with varying levels of complexity based on their distance from the camera.

- **Logical Device:** Represents an abstraction of a physical device (GPU) that applications use to submit commands and allocate resources.

M

- **Memory Heap:** A collection of memory resources available on a device. Different heaps may have different properties, such as being faster or more suitable for CPU access.

- **Mipmapping:** The process of creating multiple precomputed levels of a texture at different resolutions. This helps improve rendering performance and texture filtering quality.

- **Multi-Sampling:** A technique to reduce aliasing by sampling multiple points within each pixel. Vulkan supports **Multi-Sampling Anti-Aliasing (MSAA)**.

P

- **Pipeline:** An object that encapsulates the state required to perform rendering or compute operations. Graphics pipelines and compute pipelines are two types of pipelines.

- **Pipeline Cache:** A mechanism for storing compiled pipeline state for reuse, reducing the cost of pipeline creation.

- **Push Constant:** A small block of data that can be passed to shaders without using descriptor sets. Push constants are efficient for frequently changing data.

- **Physical Device:** Represents a physical GPU or other hardware accelerator. Applications query physical devices to determine their capabilities.

Q

- **Queue:** An object that submits commands to the GPU. Vulkan supports different types of queues, such as graphics, compute, and transfer queues.

- **Queue Family:** A group of queues that share the same capabilities. For example, a queue family may support graphics and compute operations.

R

- **Rasterization:** The process of converting geometric primitives (triangles) into fragments (pixels) that are processed by the fragment shader.

- **Render Pass:** A sequence of rendering operations that define how attachments are used and how rendering results are stored.

- **Render Target:** An image used as the output of a rendering operation, such as a color attachment.

- **Ray Tracing:** A rendering technique that simulates the way light interacts with surfaces. Vulkan supports ray tracing through dedicated extensions.

S

- **Sampler:** An object that defines how textures are sampled in shaders, including filtering and addressing modes.

- **Shader:** A program that runs on the GPU to process data. Examples include vertex shaders, fragment shaders, and compute shaders.

- **Subpass:** A portion of a render pass that allows multiple rendering operations to share the same attachments.

- **Swapchain:** A collection of images used for displaying rendered frames on the screen. The swapchain manages the process of presenting images.

T

- **Texture:** An image used in rendering to add detail to surfaces. Textures can be 2D, 3D, or cube maps.

- **Thread:** A single execution unit in a shader program. In compute shaders, multiple threads work together within a workgroup.

- **Tiling:** The process of dividing rendering operations into smaller regions (tiles) to improve performance.

V

- **Validation Layers:** Layers that check for errors and provide debugging information during development. These are essential for catching issues early in the development process.

- **Vertex Buffer:** A buffer that stores vertex data, such as positions, normals, and texture coordinates.

- **Viewport:** The region of the framebuffer that the final image is mapped to during rendering.

- **Vulkan SDK:** A collection of tools, libraries, and documentation for developing Vulkan applications. It includes validation layers, compilers, and debugging tools.

W

- **Winding Order:** The order in which vertices are defined for a triangle. The winding order determines the front face of a triangle.

- **Workgroup:** A group of threads in a compute shader that execute together. Each workgroup has a unique ID and can share local memory.

- **Write-Only:** A type of memory access where a resource can only be written to, not read from. Some Vulkan resources are designed for write-only access to optimize performance.

Z

- **Z-Buffer (Depth Buffer):** A buffer that stores depth values for each pixel. The Z-buffer is used to determine which objects are visible in a 3D scene.

Resources for Further Learning

EXPANDING YOUR KNOWLEDGE of Vulkan beyond this book is crucial for mastering the API and keeping up with advancements in graphics programming. Vulkan is an ever-evolving API with a vibrant ecosystem of tools, communities, tutorials, and official resources. This section provides a curated list of resources, including documentation, tutorials, tools, libraries, and online communities that will help you deepen your understanding and skills in Vulkan.

Official Documentation and Specifications

1. Vulkan Specification

THE **Vulkan Specification** is the definitive source for understanding the API's details. It provides a complete, detailed, and formal description of Vulkan's functionality.

- **Link:** https://www.vulkan.org/specification

While the specification can be dense, it is an invaluable resource for developers who want a complete understanding of how Vulkan works. The spec is frequently updated with each new Vulkan version and extension.

2. Vulkan API Reference

THE **Vulkan API Reference** contains detailed descriptions of each function, structure, and constant in the Vulkan API. It is essential for quick lookups while developing.

- **Link:** https://registry.khronos.org/vulkan/specs/1.3-extensions/man/html/

The API reference is structured to allow easy navigation between related concepts and functions. Bookmark this resource for everyday use.

3. Vulkan Guide

THE **Vulkan Guide** is an approachable resource for developers who are getting started with Vulkan or need clarification on best practices.

- **Link:**https://github.com/KhronosGroup/Vulkan-Guide

The Vulkan Guide offers practical insights, including how to use specific features, common pitfalls, and tips for optimization.

Tutorials and Learning Resources

1. Vulkan Tutorial by Alexander Overvoorde

THIS TUTORIAL IS ONE of the most popular and comprehensive introductions to Vulkan. It covers the essentials, from setting up a project to rendering a complete 3D scene.

- **Link:**https://vulkan-tutorial.com/

The tutorial includes example code and explanations for each step. Topics include:

- Instance and device creation

- Swapchains and framebuffers
- Graphics pipelines
- Shaders and descriptor sets
- Synchronization mechanisms

The code examples are written in C++ and designed to be accessible for beginners.

2. Learn Vulkan by Sascha Willems

SASCHA WILLEMS' **Learn Vulkan** repository is a collection of code samples demonstrating Vulkan's key features and techniques.

- **Link:**https://github.com/SaschaWillems/Vulkan

These examples cover a wide range of topics, including:

- Basic rendering
- Compute shaders
- Deferred shading
- Ray tracing
- Dynamic rendering

Each sample is well-documented and comes with a working implementation that you can build and run.

3. Vulkan Game Engine Development by Brandon Foltz

THIS SERIES FOCUSES on using Vulkan to create a simple game engine. It's ideal for those interested in applying Vulkan in game development.

- **Link:**https://www.youtube.com/playlist?list=PL8327DO66nu9qYVK7eO9RTZmQqToGxRKo

The video series is organized into digestible segments, making it easier to follow along.

Books on Vulkan

1. Vulkan Programming Guide

BY GRAHAM SELLERS, John Kessenich, and Dave Shreiner

Often referred to as the "**Vulkan Red Book,**" this guide provides a thorough introduction to Vulkan, with practical examples and detailed explanations.

- **ISBN:** 978-0134464541

2. Vulkan Cookbook

BY PAWEL LAPINSKI

This book provides a recipe-based approach to solving common tasks in Vulkan. Each chapter focuses on specific topics, providing clear solutions with code samples.

- **ISBN:** 978-1786468154

3. Real-Time Rendering

BY TOMAS AKENINE-MÖLLER, Eric Haines, and Naty Hoffman

Though not Vulkan-specific, this book covers fundamental and advanced graphics rendering techniques, many of which are applicable to Vulkan development.

- **ISBN:** 978-1138627000

Online Courses and Video Resources

1. Udacity's Advanced Graphics with Vulkan

THIS COURSE COVERS advanced concepts in graphics programming using Vulkan. It includes hands-on projects to apply what you've learned.

- **Link:** https://www.udacity.com/course/advanced-graphics-with-vulkan—ud210

2. Pluralsight: Vulkan Fundamentals

A STRUCTURED COURSE covering the basics of Vulkan, including setting up a project, understanding the pipeline, and rendering simple scenes.

- **Link:** https://www.pluralsight.com/courses/vulkan-fundamentals

---

Tools for Vulkan Development

1. Vulkan SDK

THE VULKAN SDK IS THE official set of tools, libraries, and documentation for Vulkan development. It includes:

- **Validation Layers**
- **Shader Compilers** (such as glslangValidator)
- **Debugging Tools**
- **Download Link:** https://vulkan.lunarg.com/sdk/home

2. RenderDoc

RENDERDOC IS A POPULAR open-source graphics debugger that supports Vulkan. It allows you to capture frames, inspect draw calls, and debug rendering issues.

- **Link:**https://renderdoc.org/

3. NVIDIA Nsight Graphics

A POWERFUL TOOL FOR debugging and profiling Vulkan applications. Nsight Graphics helps analyze performance and identify bottlenecks.

- **Link:**https://developer.nvidia.com/nsight-graphics

4. AMD Radeon GPU Profiler (RGP)

RGP PROVIDES DETAILED performance analysis for Vulkan applications running on AMD GPUs.

- **Link:** https://gpuopen.com/rgp/

Libraries and Frameworks

1. VMA (Vulkan Memory Allocator)

A LIBRARY THAT SIMPLIFIES memory management in Vulkan. It abstracts away the complexity of Vulkan's memory allocation API.

- **Link:**https://github.com/GPUOpen-LibrariesAndSDKs/VulkanMemoryAllocator

2. GLFW

A LIBRARY FOR CREATING windows, handling input, and managing contexts in Vulkan applications.

- **Link:**https://www.glfw.org/

3. GLM (OpenGL Mathematics)

A C++ MATHEMATICS LIBRARY designed for graphics programming. It's useful for handling vectors, matrices, and transformations.

- **Link:**https://github.com/g-truc/glm

Online Communities and Forums

1. Vulkan Subreddit

A COMMUNITY OF VULKAN developers sharing tips, news, and projects.

- **Link:**https://www.reddit.com/r/vulkan/

2. Khronos Forums

THE OFFICIAL KHRONOS forums for discussing Vulkan-related topics.

- **Link:** https://community.khronos.org/

3. Stack Overflow

USE THE [**Vulkan**] tag on Stack Overflow to ask questions and find answers to common issues.

- **Link:**https://stackoverflow.com/questions/tagged/vulkan

By leveraging these resources, you can continue to expand your knowledge and skills, stay up-to-date with the latest developments, and become a proficient Vulkan developer.

Sample Projects and Code Snippets

THIS SECTION PROVIDES a comprehensive collection of sample projects and code snippets to help you understand how to implement key concepts in Vulkan. These examples range from basic setup and initialization to more complex rendering and compute operations. Each code snippet includes explanations to guide you through the steps. You can use these as starting points for your own projects or as references when learning new aspects of Vulkan.

1. Initializing Vulkan

BEFORE YOU CAN USE Vulkan, you need to initialize the API and set up a basic Vulkan instance.

Creating a Vulkan Instance

```
#INCLUDE <VULKAN/VULKAN.h>

#include <iostream>

VkInstance createInstance() {

VkInstance instance;

VkApplicationInfo appInfo = {};

appInfo.sType = VK_STRUCTURE_TYPE_APPLICATION_INFO;

appInfo.pApplicationName = "Hello Vulkan";

appInfo.applicationVersion = VK_MAKE_VERSION(1, 0, 0);

appInfo.pEngineName = "No Engine";
```

```
appInfo.engineVersion = VK_MAKE_VERSION(1, 0, 0);
appInfo.apiVersion = VK_API_VERSION_1_0;
VkInstanceCreateInfo createInfo = {};
createInfo.sType =
VK_STRUCTURE_TYPE_INSTANCE_CREATE_INFO;
createInfo.pApplicationInfo = &appInfo;
if (vkCreateInstance(&createInfo, nullptr, &instance) !=
VK_SUCCESS) {
std::cerr << "Failed to create Vulkan instance!" << std::endl;
} else {
std::cout << "Vulkan instance created successfully!" << std::endl;
}
return instance;
}
int main() {
VkInstance instance = createInstance();
vkDestroyInstance(instance, nullptr);
return 0;
}
```

Explanation:

1. **VkApplicationInfo** contains metadata about the application, such as its name and Vulkan version.
2. **VkInstanceCreateInfo** specifies the details for creating the instance.
3. The **vkCreateInstance** function initializes the Vulkan instance.
4. Always clean up resources with **vkDestroyInstance**.

---

2. Setting Up a Vulkan Device

TO INTERACT WITH THE GPU, you need to select a physical device and create a logical device.

Selecting a Physical Device

```
VKPHYSICALDEVICE
SELECTPHYSICALDEVICE(VkInstance instance) {

uint32_t deviceCount = 0;

vkEnumeratePhysicalDevices(instance, &deviceCount, nullptr);

if (deviceCount == 0) {

std::cerr << "No GPUs with Vulkan support found!" << std::endl;

return VK_NULL_HANDLE;

}

std::vector<VkPhysicalDevice> devices(deviceCount);
```

```
vkEnumeratePhysicalDevices(instance, &deviceCount, devices.data());

for (const auto& device : devices) {

VkPhysicalDeviceProperties properties;

vkGetPhysicalDeviceProperties(device, &properties);

std::cout << "Found GPU: " << properties.deviceName << std::endl;

return device; // For simplicity, return the first device found

}

return VK_NULL_HANDLE;

}
```

Creating a Logical Device

```
VKDEVICE CREATELOGICALDEVICE(VkPhysicalDevice physicalDevice) {

VkDevice device;

float queuePriority = 1.0f;

VkDeviceQueueCreateInfo queueCreateInfo = {};

queueCreateInfo.sType = VK_STRUCTURE_TYPE_DEVICE_QUEUE_CREATE_INFO;

queueCreateInfo.queueFamilyIndex = 0;

queueCreateInfo.queueCount = 1;
```

```
queueCreateInfo.pQueuePriorities = &queuePriority;

VkDeviceCreateInfo createInfo = {};

createInfo.sType =
VK_STRUCTURE_TYPE_DEVICE_CREATE_INFO;

createInfo.queueCreateInfoCount = 1;

createInfo.pQueueCreateInfos = &queueCreateInfo;

if (vkCreateDevice(physicalDevice, &createInfo, nullptr, &device)
!= VK_SUCCESS) {

std::cerr << "Failed to create logical device!" << std::endl;

} else {

std::cout << "Logical device created successfully!" << std::endl;

}

return device;

}
```

Explanation:

1. **vkEnumeratePhysicalDevices** lists all GPUs that support Vulkan.
2. **VkDeviceQueueCreateInfo** specifies the queues you want to create.
3. **vkCreateDevice** creates a logical device to interface with the physical GPU.

3. Creating a Swapchain

A SWAPCHAIN IS A COLLECTION of images used for presenting rendered frames to the screen.

Creating the Swapchain

```
VKSWAPCHAINKHR CREATESWAPCHAIN(VkDevice device, VkSurfaceKHR surface, VkExtent2D extent) {

VkSwapchainKHR swapchain;

VkSwapchainCreateInfoKHR createInfo = {};

createInfo.sType = VK_STRUCTURE_TYPE_SWAPCHAIN_CREATE_INFO_KHR;

createInfo.surface = surface;

createInfo.minImageCount = 2; // Double buffering

createInfo.imageFormat = VK_FORMAT_B8G8R8A8_SRGB;

createInfo.imageColorSpace = VK_COLOR_SPACE_SRGB_NONLINEAR_KHR;

createInfo.imageExtent = extent;

createInfo.imageArrayLayers = 1;

createInfo.imageUsage = VK_IMAGE_USAGE_COLOR_ATTACHMENT_BIT;

createInfo.imageSharingMode = VK_SHARING_MODE_EXCLUSIVE;
```

```
createInfo.preTransform = VK_SURFACE_TRANSFORM_IDENTITY_BIT_KHR;

createInfo.compositeAlpha = VK_COMPOSITE_ALPHA_OPAQUE_BIT_KHR;

createInfo.presentMode = VK_PRESENT_MODE_FIFO_KHR;

createInfo.clipped = VK_TRUE;

if (vkCreateSwapchainKHR(device, &createInfo, nullptr, &swapchain) != VK_SUCCESS) {

std::cerr << "Failed to create swapchain!" << std::endl;

} else {

std::cout << "Swapchain created successfully!" << std::endl;

}

return swapchain;

}
```

Explanation:

1. The **VkSwapchainCreateInfoKHR** struct contains parameters like the image format, extent, and presentation mode.
2. **minImageCount** specifies the number of images in the swapchain (2 for double buffering).
3. **vkCreateSwapchainKHR** creates the swapchain.

---

4. Rendering a Triangle

ONE OF THE SIMPLEST Vulkan programs is rendering a triangle. Here's a high-level overview of the steps required.

Pipeline Setup

BEFORE RENDERING, YOU need to set up the graphics pipeline:

1. **Load Shaders** – Compile GLSL shaders into SPIR-V.
2. **Create Shader Modules** – Load SPIR-V bytecode.
3. **Define Pipeline States** – Viewport, rasterizer, color blending.
4. **Create Pipeline** – Combine all stages into a pipeline.

Rendering Commands

VOID RECORDCOMMANDBUFFER(VkCommandBuffer commandBuffer, VkPipeline pipeline, VkFramebuffer framebuffer, VkRenderPass renderPass, VkExtent2D extent) {

VkCommandBufferBeginInfo beginInfo = {};

beginInfo.sType = VK_STRUCTURE_TYPE_COMMAND_BUFFER_BEGIN_INFO;

vkBeginCommandBuffer(commandBuffer, &beginInfo);

VkRenderPassBeginInfo renderPassInfo = {};

renderPassInfo.sType = VK_STRUCTURE_TYPE_RENDER_PASS_BEGIN_INFO;

renderPassInfo.renderPass = renderPass;

```
renderPassInfo.framebuffer = framebuffer;

renderPassInfo.renderArea.offset = {0, 0};

renderPassInfo.renderArea.extent = extent;

VkClearValue clearColor = {0.0f, 0.0f, 0.0f, 1.0f};

renderPassInfo.clearValueCount = 1;

renderPassInfo.pClearValues = &clearColor;

vkCmdBeginRenderPass(commandBuffer, &renderPassInfo,
VK_SUBPASS_CONTENTS_INLINE);

vkCmdBindPipeline(commandBuffer,
VK_PIPELINE_BIND_POINT_GRAPHICS, pipeline);

vkCmdDraw(commandBuffer, 3, 1, 0, 0); // Draw a triangle

vkCmdEndRenderPass(commandBuffer);

vkEndCommandBuffer(commandBuffer);

}
```

Explanation:

1. **vkBeginCommandBuffer** starts recording commands.
2. **vkCmdBeginRenderPass** begins a render pass with clear color.
3. **vkCmdBindPipeline** binds the graphics pipeline.
4. **vkCmdDraw** issues the draw call for the triangle (3 vertices).
5. **vkCmdEndRenderPass** ends the render pass.
6. **vkEndCommandBuffer** finishes recording.

THESE EXAMPLES ILLUSTRATE essential Vulkan concepts and provide a foundation for further exploration. Each snippet is designed to be extended as you build more complex applications.

API Reference Guide

THIS SECTION PROVIDES a detailed reference guide to essential Vulkan API functions, structures, and enumerations. The goal is to give you a quick yet comprehensive overview of the critical parts of Vulkan to help streamline development. Each subsection covers a particular category of Vulkan functions and includes explanations and example usage where relevant.

1. Instance and Device Creation

vkCreateInstance

CREATES A VULKAN INSTANCE.

Prototype:

VkResult vkCreateInstance(

const VkInstanceCreateInfo* pCreateInfo,

const VkAllocationCallbacks* pAllocator,

VkInstance* pInstance);

Parameters:

- **pCreateInfo**: A pointer to a VkInstanceCreateInfo structure specifying the creation parameters.

- **pAllocator**: A pointer to custom memory allocation callbacks (can be nullptr).

- **pInstance**: A pointer to a VkInstance handle where the created instance will be stored.

Example:

```
VkInstanceCreateInfo createInfo = {};

createInfo.sType = VK_STRUCTURE_TYPE_INSTANCE_CREATE_INFO;

createInfo.pApplicationInfo = &appInfo;

VkInstance instance;

if (vkCreateInstance(&createInfo, nullptr, &instance) != VK_SUCCESS) {

std::cerr << "Failed to create instance!" << std::endl;

}
```

vkDestroyInstance

DESTROYS A VULKAN INSTANCE.

Prototype:

```
void vkDestroyInstance(

VkInstance instance,

const VkAllocationCallbacks* pAllocator);
```

Example:

```
vkDestroyInstance(instance, nullptr);
```

2. Physical Device Enumeration

vkEnumeratePhysicalDevices

LISTS THE PHYSICAL devices (GPUs) available on the system.

Prototype:

```
VkResult vkEnumeratePhysicalDevices(
VkInstance instance,
uint32_t* pPhysicalDeviceCount,
VkPhysicalDevice* pPhysicalDevices);
```

Parameters:

- **instance**: The Vulkan instance.
- **pPhysicalDeviceCount**: A pointer to the number of physical devices.
- **pPhysicalDevices**: A pointer to an array to store the physical devices.

Example:

```
uint32_t deviceCount = 0;
vkEnumeratePhysicalDevices(instance, &deviceCount, nullptr);
std::vector<VkPhysicalDevice> devices(deviceCount);
```

```
vkEnumeratePhysicalDevices(instance, &deviceCount, devices.data());
```

3. Logical Device Creation

vkCreateDevice

CREATES A LOGICAL DEVICE for interacting with a physical device.

Prototype:

```
VkResult vkCreateDevice(
VkPhysicalDevice physicalDevice,
const VkDeviceCreateInfo* pCreateInfo,
const VkAllocationCallbacks* pAllocator,
VkDevice* pDevice);
```

Example:

```
VkDeviceCreateInfo createInfo = {};
createInfo.sType = VK_STRUCTURE_TYPE_DEVICE_CREATE_INFO;
VkDevice device;
if (vkCreateDevice(physicalDevice, &createInfo, nullptr, &device) != VK_SUCCESS) {
std::cerr << "Failed to create logical device!" << std::endl;
}
```

vkDestroyDevice

DESTROYS A LOGICAL device.

Prototype:

void vkDestroyDevice(

VkDevice device,

const VkAllocationCallbacks* pAllocator);

Example:

vkDestroyDevice(device, nullptr);

---

4. Queues

vkGetDeviceQueue

RETRIEVES A HANDLE to a device queue.

Prototype:

void vkGetDeviceQueue(

VkDevice device,

uint32_t queueFamilyIndex,

uint32_t queueIndex,

VkQueue* pQueue);

Example:

VkQueue graphicsQueue;

vkGetDeviceQueue(device, queueFamilyIndex, 0, &graphicsQueue);

5. Swapchain Management

vkCreateSwapchainKHR

CREATES A SWAPCHAIN for presenting images to the screen.

Prototype:

VkResult vkCreateSwapchainKHR(

VkDevice device,

const VkSwapchainCreateInfoKHR* pCreateInfo,

const VkAllocationCallbacks* pAllocator,

VkSwapchainKHR* pSwapchain);

Example:

VkSwapchainCreateInfoKHR swapchainCreateInfo = {};

swapchainCreateInfo.sType = VK_STRUCTURE_TYPE_SWAPCHAIN_CREATE_INFO_KHR;

VkSwapchainKHR swapchain;

if (vkCreateSwapchainKHR(device, &swapchainCreateInfo, nullptr, &swapchain) != VK_SUCCESS) {

std::cerr << "Failed to create swapchain!" << std::endl;

}

vkDestroySwapchainKHR

DESTROYS A SWAPCHAIN.

Prototype:

void vkDestroySwapchainKHR(

VkDevice device,

VkSwapchainKHR swapchain,

const VkAllocationCallbacks* pAllocator);

Example:

vkDestroySwapchainKHR(device, swapchain, nullptr);

6. Command Buffers

vkAllocateCommandBuffers

ALLOCATES COMMAND BUFFERS from a command pool.

Prototype:

VkResult vkAllocateCommandBuffers(

VkDevice device,

const VkCommandBufferAllocateInfo* pAllocateInfo,

VkCommandBuffer* pCommandBuffers);

Example:

VkCommandBufferAllocateInfo allocInfo = {};

allocInfo.sType = VK_STRUCTURE_TYPE_COMMAND_BUFFER_ALLOCATE_INI

allocInfo.commandPool = commandPool;

allocInfo.level = VK_COMMAND_BUFFER_LEVEL_PRIMARY;

allocInfo.commandBufferCount = 1;

VkCommandBuffer commandBuffer;

vkAllocateCommandBuffers(device, &allocInfo, &commandBuffer);

vkBeginCommandBuffer

BEGINS RECORDING A command buffer.

Prototype:

VkResult vkBeginCommandBuffer(

VkCommandBuffer commandBuffer,

const VkCommandBufferBeginInfo* pBeginInfo);

Example:

VkCommandBufferBeginInfo beginInfo = {};

beginInfo.sType = VK_STRUCTURE_TYPE_COMMAND_BUFFER_BEGIN_INFO;

vkBeginCommandBuffer(commandBuffer, &beginInfo);

vkEndCommandBuffer

ENDS RECORDING A COMMAND buffer.

Prototype:

VkResult vkEndCommandBuffer(VkCommandBuffer commandBuffer);

Example:

vkEndCommandBuffer(commandBuffer);

7. Synchronization

vkCreateSemaphore

CREATES A SEMAPHORE for synchronization.

Prototype:

VkResult vkCreateSemaphore(

VkDevice device,

const VkSemaphoreCreateInfo* pCreateInfo,

const VkAllocationCallbacks* pAllocator,

VkSemaphore* pSemaphore);

Example:

VkSemaphoreCreateInfo semaphoreInfo = {};

semaphoreInfo.sType = VK_STRUCTURE_TYPE_SEMAPHORE_CREATE_INFO;

```
VkSemaphore imageAvailableSemaphore;

if (vkCreateSemaphore(device, &semaphoreInfo, nullptr, &imageAvailableSemaphore) != VK_SUCCESS) {

std::cerr << "Failed to create semaphore!" << std::endl;

}
```

vkDestroySemaphore

DESTROYS A SEMAPHORE.

Prototype:

```
void vkDestroySemaphore(

VkDevice device,

VkSemaphore semaphore,

const VkAllocationCallbacks* pAllocator);
```

Example:

```
vkDestroySemaphore(device, imageAvailableSemaphore, nullptr);
```

8. Cleanup Functions

ALWAYS ENSURE THAT Vulkan objects are cleaned up to avoid memory leaks. Here's a quick summary of cleanup functions:

- **vkDestroyInstance** – Cleans up the Vulkan instance.
- **vkDestroyDevice** – Cleans up the logical device.

- **vkDestroySwapchainKHR** – Cleans up the swapchain.
- **vkDestroySemaphore** – Cleans up semaphores.
- **vkDestroyCommandPool** – Cleans up command pools.

Example Cleanup Code:

```
vkDestroySemaphore(device, imageAvailableSemaphore, nullptr);

vkDestroySwapchainKHR(device, swapchain, nullptr);

vkDestroyDevice(device, nullptr);

vkDestroyInstance(instance, nullptr);
```

This API reference guide covers the core Vulkan functions necessary for most applications. As you develop more complex projects, refer to the full Vulkan specification and documentation for advanced features and best practices.

Frequently Asked Questions

THIS SECTION ADDRESSES some of the most common questions developers encounter when working with Vulkan. These FAQs cover a range of topics, from setup and debugging to performance optimization and best practices. Each question includes a detailed answer and, where applicable, relevant code snippets to illustrate solutions.

1. How do I set up a basic Vulkan application?

SETTING UP A BASIC Vulkan application involves several key steps. Here's a brief outline of the process:

1. **Create a Vulkan Instance**: Initialize the Vulkan API by creating a VkInstance.
2. **Select a Physical Device**: Enumerate the available GPUs and select one that supports Vulkan.
3. **Create a Logical Device**: Create a VkDevice to interact with the GPU.
4. **Set Up Swapchain**: Create a swapchain to manage the images used for presentation.
5. **Create Command Buffers**: Allocate and record command buffers with rendering commands.
6. **Render Loop**: Submit command buffers to the GPU in a loop and present the results.

Example Initialization Code:

VkInstance instance = createInstance();

VkPhysicalDevice physicalDevice = selectPhysicalDevice(instance);

VkDevice device = createLogicalDevice(physicalDevice);

VkSwapchainKHR swapchain = createSwapchain(device, surface, extent);

VkCommandBuffer commandBuffer = allocateCommandBuffer(device, commandPool);

---

2. Why do I need to use validation layers?

VALIDATION LAYERS are essential during development because they help catch errors and provide detailed debugging information. They validate your Vulkan API usage against the specification and can detect issues such as:

- Memory leaks

- Invalid API calls
- Resource mismanagement
- Synchronization issues

To enable validation layers, modify your VkInstanceCreateInfo during instance creation.

Example:

```
const char* validationLayers[] = {

"VK_LAYER_KHRONOS_validation"

};

VkInstanceCreateInfo createInfo = {};

createInfo.sType = VK_STRUCTURE_TYPE_INSTANCE_CREATE_INFO;

createInfo.enabledLayerCount = 1;

createInfo.ppEnabledLayerNames = validationLayers;
```

Make sure the **Vulkan SDK** is installed and the VK_LAYER_KHRONOS_validation layer is available.

3. How do I handle synchronization in Vulkan?

SYNCHRONIZATION IN Vulkan ensures that operations are executed in the correct order. Common synchronization primitives include:

1. **Semaphores**: Used to synchronize between queue operations (e.g., image acquisition and rendering).

2. **Fences**: Used to synchronize GPU work with the CPU (e.g., ensuring a frame has finished rendering).
3. **Barriers**: Used to synchronize memory accesses between different stages of the pipeline.

Example Semaphore Creation:

```
VkSemaphoreCreateInfo semaphoreInfo = {};

semaphoreInfo.sType = VK_STRUCTURE_TYPE_SEMAPHORE_CREATE_INFO;

VkSemaphore imageAvailableSemaphore;

if (vkCreateSemaphore(device, &semaphoreInfo, nullptr, &imageAvailableSemaphore) != VK_SUCCESS) {

std::cerr << "Failed to create semaphore!" << std::endl;

}
```

Example Fence Creation:

```
VkFenceCreateInfo fenceInfo = {};

fenceInfo.sType = VK_STRUCTURE_TYPE_FENCE_CREATE_INFO;

fenceInfo.flags = VK_FENCE_CREATE_SIGNALED_BIT;

VkFence renderFinishedFence;

if (vkCreateFence(device, &fenceInfo, nullptr, &renderFinishedFence) != VK_SUCCESS) {

std::cerr << "Failed to create fence!" << std::endl;

}
```

4. What are command buffers and how do they work?

COMMAND BUFFERS are containers for recording GPU commands. In Vulkan, you must record commands into command buffers before submitting them to a queue for execution.

Steps to Use Command Buffers:

1. **Allocate** command buffers from a command pool.
2. **Begin Recording** with vkBeginCommandBuffer.
3. **Record Commands** (e.g., draw calls, pipeline state changes).
4. **End Recording** with vkEndCommandBuffer.
5. **Submit** the command buffer to a queue for execution.

Example Command Buffer Allocation:

```
VkCommandBufferAllocateInfo allocInfo = {};

allocInfo.sType = VK_STRUCTURE_TYPE_COMMAND_BUFFER_ALLOCATE_INI

allocInfo.commandPool = commandPool;

allocInfo.level = VK_COMMAND_BUFFER_LEVEL_PRIMARY;

allocInfo.commandBufferCount = 1;

VkCommandBuffer commandBuffer;

vkAllocateCommandBuffers(device, &allocInfo, &commandBuffer);
```

Recording Commands:

```
VkCommandBufferBeginInfo beginInfo = {};
```

```
beginInfo.sType =
VK_STRUCTURE_TYPE_COMMAND_BUFFER_BEGIN_INFO;

vkBeginCommandBuffer(commandBuffer, &beginInfo);

// Record draw commands here

vkEndCommandBuffer(commandBuffer);
```

5. How do I debug Vulkan applications effectively?

DEBUGGING VULKAN APPLICATIONS can be challenging due to its low-level nature. Here are some effective strategies:

1. **Enable Validation Layers**: They catch API misuses and provide detailed error messages.
2. **Use Debug Callbacks**: Set up a callback function to receive debug messages from validation layers.
3. **RenderDoc**: An open-source tool for frame capture and analysis.
4. **NVIDIA Nsight Graphics**: A powerful tool for debugging and profiling.
5. **AMD Radeon GPU Profiler (RGP)**: For profiling applications on AMD hardware.

Setting Up a Debug Callback:

```
VkDebugUtilsMessengerCreateInfoEXT debugCreateInfo = {};

debugCreateInfo.sType =
VK_STRUCTURE_TYPE_DEBUG_UTILS_MESSENGER_CREA

debugCreateInfo.messageSeverity =
VK_DEBUG_UTILS_MESSAGE_SEVERITY_WARNING_BIT_E
```

```
|
VK_DEBUG_UTILS_MESSAGE_SEVERITY_ERROR_BIT_EXT;

debugCreateInfo.messageType =
VK_DEBUG_UTILS_MESSAGE_TYPE_GENERAL_BIT_EXT
|
VK_DEBUG_UTILS_MESSAGE_TYPE_VALIDATION_BIT_EXT;

debugCreateInfo.pfnUserCallback = debugCallback;

VkDebugUtilsMessengerEXT debugMessenger;

if (CreateDebugUtilsMessengerEXT(instance, &debugCreateInfo,
nullptr, &debugMessenger) != VK_SUCCESS) {

std::cerr << "Failed to set up debug messenger!" << std::endl;

}
```

6. How do I handle different platforms in Vulkan?

VULKAN IS DESIGNED for cross-platform development. To support multiple platforms (Windows, Linux, macOS, Android), follow these best practices:

1. **Platform-Specific Extensions**: Use platform-specific extensions such as VK_KHR_win32_surface for Windows or VK_KHR_xcb_surface for Linux.
2. **Conditional Compilation**: Use preprocessor directives to handle platform-specific code.

Example:

```
#ifdef _WIN32

VkWin32SurfaceCreateInfoKHR createInfo = {};
```

```
createInfo.sType =
VK_STRUCTURE_TYPE_WIN32_SURFACE_CREATE_INFO_KH

createInfo.hinstance = GetModuleHandle(nullptr);

createInfo.hwnd = hwnd;

vkCreateWin32SurfaceKHR(instance, &createInfo, nullptr,
&surface);

#elif defined(__linux__)

VkXcbSurfaceCreateInfoKHR createInfo = {};

createInfo.sType =
VK_STRUCTURE_TYPE_XCB_SURFACE_CREATE_INFO_KHR

createInfo.connection = connection;

createInfo.window = window;

vkCreateXcbSurfaceKHR(instance, &createInfo, nullptr,
&surface);

#endif
```

7. How can I optimize Vulkan performance?

PERFORMANCE OPTIMIZATION in Vulkan involves several strategies:

1. **Minimize State Changes**: Reduce pipeline and descriptor set changes during rendering.
2. **Batch Draw Calls**: Group similar draw calls to reduce overhead.
3. **Efficient Memory Management**: Use the Vulkan Memory Allocator (VMA) to manage GPU memory efficiently.

4. **Parallel Processing**: Utilize multiple threads for command buffer recording.
5. **Use Pipeline Caches**: Store compiled pipelines for reuse to reduce pipeline creation time.

Example of Using a Pipeline Cache:

```
VkPipelineCacheCreateInfo cacheInfo = {};

cacheInfo.sType = VK_STRUCTURE_TYPE_PIPELINE_CACHE_CREATE_INFO;

VkPipelineCache pipelineCache;

vkCreatePipelineCache(device, &cacheInfo, nullptr, &pipelineCache);
```

8. How do I implement compute shaders in Vulkan?

COMPUTE SHADERS ALLOW you to perform general-purpose computations on the GPU. Here are the steps to set up a compute shader:

1. **Create a Compute Pipeline.**
2. **Create a Descriptor Set** to pass data to the shader.
3. **Record Commands** to dispatch the compute shader.

Example Compute Shader Dispatch:

```
vkCmdBindPipeline(commandBuffer, VK_PIPELINE_BIND_POINT_COMPUTE, computePipeline);
```

```
vkCmdBindDescriptorSets(commandBuffer,
VK_PIPELINE_BIND_POINT_COMPUTE, pipelineLayout, 0,
1, &descriptorSet, 0, nullptr);

vkCmdDispatch(commandBuffer, workGroupX, workGroupY,
workGroupZ);
```

This FAQ section addresses key challenges and common tasks in Vulkan development. Use these solutions as references to streamline your workflow and avoid common pitfalls.

www.ingramcontent.com/pod-product-compliance
Lightning Source LLC
LaVergne TN
LVHW090305210926
848480LV00001B/135
9798230939351